The Murder of Laura Dickinson

Ruth Kanton

Published by Trellis Publishing, 2021.

While every precaution has been taken in the preparation of this book, the publisher assumes no responsibility for errors or omissions, or for damages resulting from the use of the information contained herein.

THE MURDER OF LAURA DICKINSON

First edition. July 11, 2021.

Copyright © 2021 Ruth Kanton.

ISBN: 979-8224815319

Written by Ruth Kanton.

THE MURDER OF LAURA DICKINSON

RUTH KANTON

Laura Leigh Dickinson

On December 12, 2006, Laura Leigh Dickinson took time off from studying, and made her way to a party hosted by the novice crew at Eastern Michigan University in Ypsilanti, Michigan. 22-year-old Laura had joined the school's nutrition program later than most of her classmates, owing to the fact that she had decided to get her Associate's Degree in nutrition from Grand Rapids Community College before she worked on her Bachelor's Degree. After enrolling in the university, Laura quickly joined the novice rowing crew as a way to keep fit, where she made fast friends. The Christmas party was hosted early, since it was finals week and crew members were just about to starting leaving school for Christmas break. She spent time talking to her friends and having fun, and gladly accepted the Christmas gift she got from her secret Santa. At 11:12 p.m., she made her way into her dormitory building, a red-and-green gift bag in her hand. Inside was what looked like a stuffed toy.

Murder

Laura lived in room 518 in Hill Hall dormitory, a single room. When she walked into her door after the secret Santa Christmas party, she called her boyfriend Travis Scott, who worked at an engineering firm, Covanta Energy, in Grand Rapids, Michigan. Scott was working late, and the two spoke for a few minutes before Laura stated that she was turning in for the night. Laura had exams the next day, and when she failed to show up, her friends increasingly grew concerned. They began frantically calling her phone, but she was not picking up. In Hastings, Michigan, Robert and Debra Dickinson, Laura's parents, were also growing concerned. They were a tight-knit family, and the phone calls were frequent. Laura always picked up her phone, and in the rare occasions that she didn't, she always returned the calls soon after. They reached out to Scott, who was having the same problems. By December 15, 2006, two days after anyone last heard from Laura, Robert and Scott began making plans to drive down to the school.

After discussing the plan, Scott decided that he would take the day off work and check on Laura, promising to call back with news as soon as he found out what was going on.

As Scott made his way towards the campus, Hill Hall custodian Michelle Lockwood received a foul odor complaint from some of the residents. She made her way to room 518, noting that the odor was stronger at the door. She unlocked the door and pushed it open, immediately noting the gruesome scene just inside the door. Laura was lying on the carpeted floor – naked from the waist down – with a pillow over her face. Immediately following the discovery, Lockwood closed the door and called campus police. She had no idea what had happened to Laura, but the odor was enough to convince her that the junior was deceased. Eastern Michigan University campus police officer Kenneth Hardesty was the first security official to respond to the scene. He made his way to Laura's room, where he confirmed that she was unresponsive. He noted the body's position and state of undress, and decided to only conduct a visual inspection at the time. He later testified that his decision was based on the fact that he "didn't want to disturb anything in the room in case it was a crime scene."

Jeffrey Nesmith, Eastern Michigan University campus police lieutenant, arrived at the scene not long after. They immediately launched an investigation into Laura's death, mainly because they suspected foul play, but hoped that it was not. Lieutenant Nesmith placed a call to the Michigan State Police Crime Lab and asked for help processing the crime scene. As the crime scene technicians documented their observations, they noticed what looked like semen on Laura's legs. They took samples, and Laura's body was transported to the county medical examiner's office. Following a cursory initial exam, the medical examiner listed Laura's death as suspicious, noting that he suspected foul play. With this, investigators began looking for Laura's killer.

University Betrays Its Community

When Laura's parents received the notification that Laura had been discovered dead in her dorm room, they immediately banded together and made the drive down to the campus. Laura's parents, Robert and Debra, her two brothers, and her boyfriend Scott were informed that she was found unresponsive in her room, and that there were no signs of foul play. Laura had been diagnosed with a heart problem when she was younger, and her family latched on to the conclusion that she had probably died of a possible heart attack or heart failure. News of Laura's death began spreading on campus, and some students began expressing concern over their own safety.

On December 16, 2006, the university posted a message regarding Laura's death on its website, assuring staff and students alike: "At this point, there is no reason to suspect foul play. We are fully confident in the safety and security of our campus environment, and our campus officials will remain vigilant in ensuring safety for all members of our campus community." The school went on to assure the students that there will be services offered to help them cope with the sudden death of one of their own. Students were encouraged to speak about how they were feeling, and services were extended to Laura's family to help with their grief. Laura's friends held a memorial for her on campus, mourning the loss of her young life. They believed she had died of heart failure, although this had not been revealed in any of the school's statements aimed at assuring the students of their safety on campus.

Despite the school's numerous assurances that there had been no foul play in Laura's death, her family harbored suspicions that they were not being apprised of the full information. Her boyfriend, Scott, was interviewed by investigators a few weeks after Laura's death, which seemed suspicious. Additionally, Laura had not shown any signs of being sick. She was healthy – despite her heart condition – was a vegetarian, and made sure she exercised regularly and was vigilant about making sure she did not indulge in habits that would worsen her condition. "We always suspected something had happened besides something natural, but we had no idea what," Robert later said. With no proof to back up their suspicions, Laura was buried and her family and friends began the process of trying to heal from their sudden loss.

However, all hell broke loose just 10 weeks after Laura's death. As students at the university settled back in school after the winter break, news broke out that Laura's death was not the untimely result of her heart condition, but a murder. On February 23, 2007, 21-year-old Orange Amir Taylor III, a student at the university, was arrested for the rape and murder of Laura Leigh Dickinson. The news was met with outrage and shock, with Laura's family feeling blindsided by the news. Laura's father, Robert, stated that the university had "lied to us. They let us bury her thinking that a healthy 22-year-old girl died by some freak accident." For the students, the betrayal cut deep. In addition to their safety being disregarded, from February 27, students could no longer withdraw from their classes or they would be penalized academically, and they could not receive a full refund if they decided to withdraw from housing. The timing of Taylor's arrest was suspicious, and many speculated that it was orchestrated by the school to ensure that they would not be mass withdrawals from housing or classes by the students.

Criticisms

Following Taylor's arrest, the university president, John A. Fallon, released a statement addressing the situation: "It was reported early on that foul play was not suspected. As the investigation developed, however, there were serious, strong, and abiding concerns about the raising of information that would prejudice the case. It affected the nature and focus and specificity of the information." As the university raced to try and contain the backlash, President Fallon decided to host various meetings with the students, faculty and community to address any concerns related to Laura's case.

In one of the public forums, Asia David, a 20-year-old student who lived a few floors above Laura, stated: "They kept telling us there was no cause for alarm; we were sleeping through this girl being murdered in her room. It just seems like they were really holding stuff back from us."

Another student, Jessica Richardson, stated: "I felt like they were really lying to us by saying that there was no foul play even suspected." The sophomore added that Taylor's arrest came as a complete shock to her because she had been told by her supervisor that Laura had committed suicide.

Jason Gardner, a student who commuted to campus, stated: "It's terrible for all the students that have to go through this. I just think whoever's responsible should be gone."

Victor Walker, another student, said: "Sometimes a few short words can make all the difference. Even if it had been 'we are not sure, but we may have a possible homicide.' I don't know anyone who's going to run out in the street howling and screaming if they say that. But then you don't walk around with your head in the clouds not believing you could fall victim to the same thing."

Student Jaclyn Armstrong echoed similar sentiments, saying in one meeting: "I was specifically told I was not in danger. That we weren't in danger. And unless you guys already had a guy in custody, we were in danger. And the fact that he is being charged with criminal sexual assault, not only were our lives in danger, but we were in danger of many other things."

Speaking to *Los Angeles Times*, Stephen Gillers, a professor of legal ethics at New York University's School of Law, stated that while he did understand that there were legitimate reasons why campus police and university officials would not comment on the details of a case, lying to Laura's parents was "an abdication of every responsibility a university administration has. There's no reason for law enforcement to fear that keeping the parents informed will frustrate the ability to apprehend the perpetrator. This is not the theft of a computer. It's the death of a child."

Investigation and Arrest

Following the discovery of Laura's body, investigators began reviewing the security footage from the camera outside Hill Hall dormitory. They watched as Laura opened the buildings front door with her set of keys, the gift bag in her hand with a stuffed toy visible at the top. The footage showed that in the early hours of December 13, 2006, a man walked up to the door and began trying to make his way in. He was finally able to gain entry into Hill Hall after he walked in behind someone who had opened the door with a key. 90 minutes later, the man exited the building and appeared to be carrying the same gift bag that Laura had been seen with as she entered the building. Investigators began looking for the man, and two weeks later, they identified him as 21-year-old Orange Amir Taylor III, who had been caught in 2005 breaking into a dorm to steal electronics. Investigators were unable to locate Laura's keys in her room during the investigation, and combined with the fact that custodian Michelle Lockwood had found the door to room 518 locked, they believed that Taylor had taken them after he left the scene of the crime.

Taylor was brought in for voluntary questioning on January 25, 2007. When he was asked whether he raped and killed Laura, he denied the accusation. With no evidence to prove the contrary, he was released. However, investigators began the process of obtaining a search warrant for Taylor's home. They found the sweatshirt he was seeing wearing on the night of the murder, and investigators were able to recover the gift bags Laura had been seen with as she left the secret Santa party on December 12, 2006. They tested the semen samples recovered from Laura's legs, comparing the DNA to Taylor's. The results were a match. Investigators were convinced that Taylor was responsible for Laura's death.

On February 28, 2007, Bader Cassin, Washtenaw County Medical Examiner, told the media that Laura's death had been ruled suspicious almost immediately. In the autopsy report, which he finalized on March 5, 2007, Cassin concluded Laura's death was as a result of "probable asphyxiation." However, the report failed to document the physical details that could have determined exactly how she died due to the fact that her body had already reached an advanced state of decomposition.

Following his arrest, Taylor was charged with open murder, larceny, home invasion, and two counts of sexual criminal conduct. He pled guilty, and was held in Washtenaw County Jail without bond. His trial was set to start in October 2007.

Trial, Sentencing and Appeal

On October 15, 2007, the trial against Orange Amir Taylor III began in Washtenaw County Court on East Huron Street. The prosecutor handling the case, Blaine Longsworth, stated in his open arguments that Taylor had killed Laura in a manner that reflected "every woman's nightmare come true." Prosecutors explained the investigation, stating that they were able to arrest Taylor because of DNA and other physical evidence. The prosecution called on various witnesses during the course of the trial, including Laura's boyfriend Travis Scott, her rowing teammate Maria Clary, as well as Michelle Lockwood, Hill Hall dormitory's custodian. Many of Laura's friends and acquaintances stated that they didn't think Laura and Taylor had crossed paths before the night of her murder.

Alvin Keel, Taylor's defense attorney, did not dispute the prosecution's assertions that Taylor had been in Laura's room on that fateful night. However, he maintained that there was no way the prosecution could prove beyond reasonable that his client was actually responsible for Laura's death. He highlighted the fact that the autopsy report stated that Laura had died from "probable asphyxia." "(The autopsy) did not say asphyxia. It simply said probable. Probable is one of those terms which does not meet the standard of guilt beyond reasonable doubt," he told the court. He also highlighted that Laura had experienced cardiac problems in 2005, and this could not be ruled out, stating that Laura may have been sick in the days leading up to her death.

Keel explained to the court that Taylor had been in a different dorm that night, smoking marijuana with a friend. He later left the room to look for more marijuana, and that is how he wandered into Laura's room. He began rummaging in the room, and didn't notice Laura at first. He maintained that his client had nothing to do with Laura's death. When Taylor saw Laura on the floor "in a compromising position," he stood over her and masturbated, ejaculating on her body. "(Physical evidence) doesn't even mean you touched the person," Keel added. He also noted that on the night of December 13, 2006, the girls in the room next to Laura had been present, and they later stated that they never heard any suspicious noises.

Taylor didn't take the stand in his own defense. On October 28, 2007, Washtenaw Circuit Court Judge Archie Brown declared a mistrial. After three days of deliberation, the jury was hopelessly deadlocked.

In December, Alvin Keel withdrew his services because Taylor's family was unable to afford his fees anymore. His case was picked up by Assistant Public Defender Laura Graham. Taylor's second trial commenced on March 31, 2008, still presided over by Circuit Court Judge Archie Brown. The prosecution stuck to its arguments from the first trial. Graham, on her part, cross-examined the prosecution's witnesses, concluding that the witnesses who had seen the crime did not witness any signs of a physical struggle. She also suggested that the evidence recovered from Laura's room could have been tainted because the individuals who entered the room to investigate were not wearing shoe covers or protective gloves. Taylor did not testify at the second trial either.

On April 7, 2008, after just a few hours of deliberation, the jury found Taylor guilty of first-degree felony murder, assault with intent to commit sexual penetration, home invasion, and larceny. During his sentencing hearing on May 7, 2008, minutes before Judge Brown passed down his sentence, Taylor maintained his innocence once more. He told the court that he may have done a number of inappropriate things, but "one thing I am not is a murderer." Despite his insistence, he was sentenced to serve mandatory life in prison without the possibility of parole for the murder of Laura Leigh Dickinson.

Laura's parents declined to speak to the court before Taylor was sentenced, but they handed over their letters to Assistant Prosecutor Blaine Longsworth, who read them out in the packed courtroom. In her letter, Debra Dickinson stated that she cried often, and that Laura's death had shaken her faith in God. She wrote that Laura was a "smiling, compassionate ray of sunshine," and that the family was going to miss her love, support, and encouragement. "You took away the gift God gave us," Debra wrote. In his letter, Robert Dickinson wrote about Laura's aspirations, and stated that she was never going to achieve them because of Taylor's actions. He wrote: "You totally destroyed my family. You tore it limb from limb. Not only did you kill Laura, you killed a very big part of me."

Taylor's mother, Tina Taylor, had told the media during her son's first trial, "We've obviously never been through anything like this before. We're hopeful that we'll get justice." However, following her son's sentencing, she watched as Taylor was walked out of the court to start his sentence. He mouthed, "I love you," at her as he was led off.

Taylor appealed his case, claiming that his lawyer had been ineffective, as she had failed to cross-examine the medical examiner. In April 2010, the Michigan Court of Appeals rejected Taylor's claims and in its decision, upheld the first-degree murder conviction.

The Clery Act

The Jeanne Clery Disclosure of Campus Security Policy and Campus Crime Statistics Act, passed in 1990, was named after Jeanne Clery, a freshman at Lehigh University who was raped, beaten, cut and murdered in her dorm room on April 5, 1986. Her killer, Josoph

M. Henry, had gained entry into Stoughton Hall where Clery lived through the door of the building, which had been propped open by boxes of pizza. Clery's room door was unlocked because her roommate had forgotten her keys, and didn't want to wake Clery up when she came back. Henry was arrested after he bragged about the murder to a couple of friends and they reported him to police.

Clery's parents, Connie and Howard Clery – the more they uncovered information regarding their daughter's murder – grew increasingly convinced that her death had been due to the "slipshod" security provided on campus. They also believed that the campus had "a rapidly escalating crime rate, which they didn't tell anybody about," even though the university's vice president at the time, John Smeaton, insisted that the school's security measures were "more than adequate, reasonable and appropriate for our setting and our situation. You can't prevent everything from happening." Despite the university's assurances, Howard and Connie founded Security on Campus, Inc., a nonprofit organization, which was later renamed the Clery Center for Security on Campus. The family pushed for better security practices on campuses, including providing information regarding crime statistics in the campuses. They maintained that if they had known about the other 37 violent crimes that had occurred on the campus – excluding Clery's attack – they would have never allowed their daughter to enroll in the school.

The Clery Act mandates all universities and colleges that are part of the federal financial aid programs recipients to record, keep, and disclose information about crime in or near their campuses. The Act provides a number of disclosure requirements, which generally fall under the following categories:

- The Clery crime statistics and security-related policy requirements – must be met by all institutions

· The Clery crime log requirement – for institutions with campus police or security departments

· The HEOA missing student notification and fire safety requirements – for institutions with at least one on-campus student housing facility.

The United States Department of Education monitors compliance, with violations incurring fines of up to $54,789 per violation, or even suspension from participating in the federal student financial aid programs.

Eastern Michigan University Clery Act Violations

As the details of Laura's murder and the school's decision to hide the details began garnering national attention, Eastern Michigan University found itself in the middle of a Department of Education Investigation into whether it violated the Clery Act of 1990. Following the conclusion of its investigation, the D.O.E released its final report on November 20, 2007. The report stated "The findings in this program review report indicate numerous andsystemic violations by EMU of the Clery Act requirements. EMU ... failed to take action to ensure the safety and wellbeing of the campus community."

The report listed seven violations uncovered during the investigation, including:

· Failure to issue a "timely warning" campus alert
· Lack of a "timely warning" policy for the campus
· Lack of capability to provide campus security
· Failure to maintain a campus crime log
· Improperly disclosing crime statistics for 2003 - 2005
· Incomplete reports of crimes
· Lack of policy on preparing crime statistics

On December 18, 2007, Eastern Michigan University was fined $357,000 for "serious, numerous and repeated" violations of the Clery Act in the cover-up of the suspected rape and murder of Laura Leigh Dickinson. This amount only slightly differed from the $357,500 fine originally proposed by D.O.E.

In a statement addressing the fine, Don Loppnow, provost and executive vice president, said: "We're pleased to have arrived at an agreement with the DOE and we appreciate their recognition of the progress and improvements that EMU has made during the past year in regards to Clery Act compliance. EMU will continue its efforts to emphasize safety and security on campus."

Aftermath

Following Taylor's arrest, Eastern Michigan University's Board of Regents began holding meetings to discuss the disciplinary action that should be taken against the school officials who decided to keep Laura's murder quiet. In the end, the board fired President John A. Fallon, Vice President of Student Affairs Jim Vick, and the Public Safety Director and Chief of Police Cindy Hall.

After his termination, of which he was notified through a letter, Fallon stated: "As a citizen, I am disappointed in this hastily called meeting, without any opportunity to be present or to respond. I have a story to tell and intend to tell it." He maintained that he had no clue about the cover-up, but no one believed him. He maintained that Vick was mainly behind the decision to keep the students, faculty, parents, and community in the dark, but some believed that Vick was just chosen as the scapegoat.

In addition to the fines imposed by the District of Education, Eastern Michigan University chose to settle the lawsuit filed against the institution by the Dickinson family. The family received $2.5 million, on the condition that the university was deemed "not liable" for Laura's death. The settlement was concluded on December 13, 2007, a year to the day Laura was murdered. Both parties released a joint statement regarding the settlement, which read:

> "Eastern Michigan University and the Family and Estate of Laura Leigh Dickinson, through their representatives, The Law Firm of GEE & LONGSTREET LLP, in Hastings, Michigan, Robert Dickinson and Debra Dickinson, Parents of Laura Leigh Dickinson, have agreed to settle for 2.5 million dollars the claim of the Family and Estate arising out of Laura Leigh Dickinson's tenure as a student at Eastern Michigan University and her unfortunate death. Eastern Michigan University has agreed to the settlement without any admission of liability on the part of the University."

Eastern Michigan University began making changes to its structure and processes in a bid to ensure that a similar scenario would not occur again. The campus increased the visibility of foot patrols, continued private security service, and implemented an emergency text alerting system. SEEUS program, which hires students to escort other students who are in campus late at night, was also launched and implemented. The university also added computerized systems in dormitories to check visitors in and out during the night watch.

KILLER HANDYMAN

JOLENE DEAN

It was February of 1955 in Toronto, Canada. The temperatures averaged sixteen degrees Fahrenheit and citizens were cozied up in their homes for the time being. At the time, immigrants were moving into the neighborhoods and what was once a quiet, peaceful city was beginning to turn into a bonafide metropolis. On the twenty-seventh of that month, a little boy was born to two parents. However, his biological father disappeared not long after his birth and was never to be heard from again. His mother struggled for three years to keep food on the table for her and her son, and then his aunt finally intervened. She being a recluse, there isn't much known about the boy's time with his aunt.

There are stories about him as a child that painted him as a quiet boy who often made other children feel uneasy, but they didn't have a specific reason as to why. When he became of age and was able to trek out on his own, he took odd jobs here and there as a traveling handyman. Unfortunately, young William was not able to stay away from a life of petty crime that quickly grew into a life of savagery.

He reconnected with his mother in his early thirties, but did not have contact with her before that point as far as the police and investigators know. Many suspect something terrible happened during William's childhood to make him who he is today, but there are no records of abuse or neglect while he was under the care of his aunt. In fact, many believe she instilled some very good qualities in him as a boy. William would not have been able to become the independent handyman he'd been in his twenties if she had not.

Despite his life of small, petty crimes, William was a successful handyman.

It was at the age of twenty-two when his life took a notable turn. According to court records and newspapers, William was convicted for several different charges. He was convicted of abduction, breaking and entering, theft, and pretending to solemnize a marriage. In addition, he was convicted of libel, or a written defamation.

The cause of this change in his behavior? William Fyfe had begun to experiment with drugs. He would later seek counseling for this addiction, but it was never clear if he actually was able to become clean or if he was just able to control his actions while he was under the influence. William would find odd jobs here and there to fuel his drug habit, and if those jobs dried up, he resorted to robbery.

After Fyfe was released for the aforementioned crimes, he began a wanderer. He lived in several different cities across Canada until he finally settled in with his biological mother.

He appeared to be a normal individual who didn't harbor any murderous tendencies, but the mother of one of his hockey buddies soon learned this was untrue. William's murderous ways began in 1979 with Hazel Scattolon, but it wouldn't be until the late nineties that he was finally arrested and charged with her death, as well as four more deaths. If these were the only crimes he'd committed, he wouldn't be considered the deadliest serial killer Canada has ever seen, but there is evidence to suggest William has been a part of numerous other crimes over the twenty years between Hazel's murder and the murders of Anna Yarnold, Monique Gaudreau, Teresa Shanahan, and Mary Glen.

If this is the case, then he would be classified as the deadliest serial killer of Canada, but unfortunately, William Fyfe is rather tight-lipped about his involvement in the open cases.

Let's explore the life of William Fyfe and what it is that made him one of Canada's most frightening criminals.

Chapter One – The Beginning of the End

William Fyfe was not pegged as a suspect for the first few murders he committed, nor was he a suspect in the serial rapes that took place in the 1980's that he later claimed he committed. What was his ultimate downfall were the murders that took place in the 1990's, beginning with a woman named Anna Yarnold.

Anna Yarnold

It was an average winter in October of 1999 for Senneville, Quebec. The neighborhood was peaceful and the police were not accustomed to handling violent crime. With around 1,500 residents, it was quite clear the occupants of this peaceful town knew one another well.

Her neighbors and living relatives described Anna Yarnold as an artistic woman who enjoyed painting and making flower arrangements. Her daughter describes her as being a spontaneous woman who was very much into life. Unfortunately, it was cut short.

In October of 1999, Anna lived in Senneville, Quebec, a quiet, peaceful area the police considered an easygoing place to work due to the little amount of violent crime they witnessed. The population was around fifteen hundred people, with the area being secluded and wooded. Mrs. Yarnold's home was located off the beaten path where the only thing to be seen from the windows were trees. Her home was private and secluded, making her an easy target, unfortunately.

The day Mrs. Yarnold was murdered was like any other day in Senneville, Quebec. Anna was worried about the health of her dog, Trooper, and took him to the local veterinarian at three in the afternoon. She'd noticed a lump on his side and was very worried about him. Her veterinarian informed her Trooper's lump could be cancerous and they had to remove it. After the appointment, Anna took Trooper home to her secluded, waterfront home.

Worried about his wife, Robert Yarnold called her from work to check in on her and Trooper shortly after they arrived home. Her daughter called her around five thirty in the afternoon and noticed her mother sounded as if she'd been crying. They talked for quite some time about Trooper, and Sarah Yarnold tried to calm her mother. Both her husband and her daughter assured her everything would be okay with Trooper, and that was the last either one of them spoke with her.

As darkness fell over the providence of Montreal, West Island, an unexpected visitor approached Anna Yarnold's home in a pickup truck. On October 15, 1999, the following morning, her daughter and husband both tried calling her multiple times because they were worried about her emotional well-being concerning Trooper. By that time, it was too late.

Both repeatedly attempted to reach the fifty-nine-year-old woman. As the evening set in on October 15, Robert Yarnold drove up this wife's home. The first thing he noticed about her home was the lights were on and her vehicle was in the driveway. Worried and curious, Robert went inside her home to look for his wife and her dog. He first searched the downstairs rooms but quickly made his way up to the upstairs bedrooms. In a guest bedroom, he found Trooper alive and well. On the bed, he found signs of possible foul play.

His wife's purse was on the spare bedroom's bed and her wallet was open. Her cards were strewn about and her change was emptied out across the bed. Worried, Robert decided to search for his wife. Finally, he made his way downstairs and out into the yard. Just outside a screened in porch near a triangular flower bed, he found his wife's body. She was lying face down, and when he turned her, it was obvious she had been murdered.

Robert Yarnold called the police, who arrived at the scene within an hour, and amongst them was a forensic photographer who took pictures of the scene. In the case file, it was noted she had bruises on her neck and around her face and severe head wounds. An officer found the flowerpot with blood caked on it and they labeled this as the murder weapon, but they were unable to get fingerprints due to the flowerpot's rough texture.

As police walked through the scene, they pieced together a possible chain of events.

Anna was attacked in her bathroom, where they found her glasses in the sink. It was clear she put up a fight, but he soon caught up with her outside and choked her before he beat her with the flowerpot. Once he was sure she was dead, he went back inside and stole what he was able to from her purse. While it appeared to be a robbery at first, police were suspicious of the obvious overkill.

When it comes to persons of interest in a case such as this, police often look at the victim's family members first. The closest family member is always the one who is scrutinized before anyone else, and in this case, it was Robert Yarnold. Robert was taken to the police station for questioning before his daughter, Sarah, was notified. She didn't know of the news yet and was called by her father around midnight.

Sarah was already worried about her mother and wanted to know what was happening, but her father wouldn't tell her over the phone. He told her was at the police station in St. Charles, and she immediately went there. She could see her father through the glass door of a conference room, but she was not able to go inside and speak with him. The police took Sarah to another room and began to ask her questions about the relationship her parents had together. Eventually, one of the officers blurted out to Sarah that her mother was dead. She describes the incident as shocking, but she didn't really believe what they were saying and couldn't believe her mother was dead. From the first moment she knew, she believed her father had not committed the crime.

Still, Robert was questioned late into the night but was only considered a person of interest at the time and not a suspect. Sarah and her father assumed it was a robbery, but the police began to say something completely different. The forensic scientist came up with absolutely nothing as they continued to search for clues. They searched her purse for fingerprints and the murder weapon. They searched the halls and the bathroom where they knew the suspect had been.

Nothing they were able to find helped them in the case of Anna Yarnold. Forensics had a difficult time finding anything that was of use because it was a murder committed by an outsider, making it difficult to look for anything that might be out of the ordinary.

Needless to say, the community was disturbed and frightened when the news was released about Anna Yarnold's death. There wasn't a clear motive as to why it happened, frightening her neighbors and those who knew her even more. She was a woman who was dearly loved in her community, and while some suspected her husband, others feared something much worse. If it was a stranger who committed this crime, then they could be next.

The police feared it was part of a much larger problem. Just three months prior, another violent incident had taken place.

Janet Kuchinsky

Somewhere in the files of the Montreal Police Station's Major Crimes Division rests a folder with the name Janet Kuchinsky. Unfortunately, her file rests in the cold case section. Janet was a forty-two-year-old mother of three who was bludgeoned to death off a bicycle path at the north end of Sources Boulevard in Pierrefonds on July 10, 1999. No one has been charged with her murder.

After six in the evening on July 10th, Jane t left her home to go out on one of her frequent walks. According to the reports, police suspect she was killed shortly after she left. Her body was found the following day. No sexual assault had taken place and theft was ruled out because there was nothing missing. During the course of the investigation, numerous tips were followed but they all led to nothing.

A twenty-thousand dollar reward was posted for information leading to the arrest of a suspect, but it went unclaimed. If the murder of Janet and Anna were connected, it would have tipped the police off to a serial killer. The police advised everyone in the area not to answer the door to people they didn't know.

In the meantime, Robert Yarnold fully cooperated with the police, but it still wasn't good enough at the time. In the weeks that followed, there were no new attacks, but two new crimes in different areas caught the police's attention.

Chapter Two – The Murder of Monique Gaudreau and Teresa Shanahan

Fyfe was just getting started when he killed Anna Yarnold. The violence of her death pales in comparison to the violence Monique Gaudreau and Teresa Shanahan experienced.

Monique Gaudreau

Monique was a forty-five-year-old nurse who worked in Sainte-Agathe-des-Monts, Quebec and was described as being kind and caring to her patients. She wasn't one to be late for work or to miss her shift. On October 29, 1999, two weeks after Anna Yarnold was murdered, Monique failed to show up for her shift. Her coworkers and employer were concerned about her whereabouts and called her home multiple times. When they were unable to reach her, they contacted her sister who decided to drive to her home that evening.

Inside, Monique's sister found a gruesome discovery. The amount of violence at the scene shocked even the most seasoned veterans. Monique had been badly beaten across the head and face, and she had been stabbed multiple times. At one point during the struggle, she had been sexually assaulted. The police were unable to determine how many stab wound had been inflicted, but they estimated over fifty. It was evident to them the killer was a very sick-minded individual.

At this murder, a biologist was called to the scene to search for clues. The forensic photographer took photographs of the excessive amount of blood scattered across the walls in order to preserve the scene before the biologist was able to begin working. The police discovered few clues inside the home despite the attack being so brutal.

They were unable to find signs of forced entry, meaning Monique had opened her door to the intruder. They did not find a murder weapon, so the murderer must have taken it with him. There were not any fingerprints, and there was nothing missing from the scene. Only when they moved to the outside landing near the front porch did their search finally pay off.

A footprint was able to be pulled from the scene. They knew it was the killer's because it was in Monique's blood. What they also discovered was droplets of blood that led away from the scene, meaning the killer had hurt himself during the altercation. Usually, when an attacker goes after a victim with that much violence, they end up slipping and cutting themselves or hurting themselves with the weapon they're using.

The biologist determined the blood belonged to a male suspect, but nothing else was able to be gleaned from the scene. Because there was not a similar cause of death, the connection between Anna and Monique were not made until William Fyfe was caught.

The police knew they were getting closer to a suspect, but they weren't close enough. The blood came up with nothing in their database.

Teresa Shanahan

On November 19, 1999, three weeks after Monique as discovered murdered, employees at a local firm in Laval, Quebec were concerned about the absence of their accountant. Teresa Shanahan was a fifty-five-year-old woman who lived alone in an apartment complex. When her coworkers and the police finally arrived at her apartment, the first thing they saw was three or four newspapers stacked in front of her door.

Suspicious, the police had the concierge open the door. What they found was as gruesome as the murder of Monique. Teresa was found dead in her apartment. Evidence suggested she had been sexually assaulted and beaten before she was stabbed thirty-two times. The murder had a striking resemblance to Monique Gaudreau's. However, there was something different about this one.

There were items missing from her apartment. Bank cards and jewelry were missing. One of her bank cards were used at an ATM shortly after her estimated time of death. The perpetrator had emptied out her savings account, making one five hundred dollar withdrawal before midnight and one after. The police immediately had the security footage from the bank confiscated to review it for a suspect.

The person they saw in the video was definitely not Teresa. It was a man, but they were only able to see him from above and behind, so identification was impossible. However, it was clear the man knew her PIN number for the bank card.

Across the providence, Sarah Yarnold was making a discovery of her own. She was skimming through her mother's financial records when she noticed something untoward. Someone had withdrawn money on the day of her mother's death. Police immediately secured a security tape from the ATM on the day of Anna Yarnold's death. The man in the video was facing the camera, but he was wearing a hood that made it difficult to determine who he was. However, the police were able to determine the man in the video was around five foot ten and Caucasian with a beard.

There was one thing that was certain. The man in the video was not Robert Yarnold, and this cleared his name from the investigation. While there was relief on Sarah and Robert's side, there was dread on the police's. They knew at this point they might be dealing with a serial killer.

It was clear to them, after discovering Teresa, that the man had used torture in order to get the women to tell him their PIN numbers for their bank cards. It was also clear to them that he picked out women at random rather than targeting them specifically. Four women had been brutally murdered in the span of six months, and they were all pointing toward this man. Based on the evidence that suggested the women had opened up their doors to this man, it was clear he was using some sort of disguise. Thus, they nicknamed him The Killer Handyman.

Even though the police knew the murders were connected, they didn't have much to go on. They had some blood samples and a footprint, but none of it pointed to anyone in particular. It wasn't until the murder of Mary Glen that they had some solid evidence.

Chapter Three – The Final Murder

Eight weeks later, on December 14, 1999, in the providence where Anna Yarnold had been murdered, a man approached one of the many large homes of Baie-D'Urfe, Quebec. He wore a working man's clothes. When a woman answered the door, he explained to her he was doing yard work in the neighborhood and wanted to offer his services. The woman consulted with her husband and the two decided not to hire him. She later realized how much of a brush with death she'd had.

The man left her home and traveled down the road, where he came to Mary Glen's home. She lived alone in a waterfront home and was employed as a graphic artist who was described as outgoing and well-known in her community. The same man who claimed to be doing yard work in the area walked up her home later on in the day.

The following morning, a housekeeper arrived at the home to perform her scheduled duties. After she had tried multiple times to attract Mary's attention to open the door, she entered the home and found Mary dead in the living room in a pool of her own blood. The police arrived soon after.

Mary had been beaten, stabbed, and sexually assaulted just as the other two women. She'd been beaten in the face with a blunt object and had been stabbed several times. After the forensic photographer had been finished preserving the scene with photo and video, the biologist was called in again. She performed blood stain analysis and projection to determine how the murder played out.

By studying the blood trail, they were able to put together a sequence of events for the attack. There were no signs of forced entry, suggesting Mary opened the door to her attacker. The attack began in the kitchen, where it was very violent. It moved into the side office where evidence showed Mary had succeeded in escaping several times. There were clumps of hair that had been violently ripped out, suggesting she'd tried to escape.

At the bottom of the stairs, the investigators found her bloody glasses. There were also pieces of hair with blood on them there, too. The murder finally ended in the living room where it was very violent and messy.

Investigators discovered faint footprints in the blood that were different from the one's found at Monique's home. The killer had gone back to the steps from the living room to the kitchen, where there was diluted blood in the sink. It was at this point he either washed his hands or he washed something off in the sink. He'd gone to the second floor where police discovered footprints from the killer on the stairs. He'd searched a few rooms upstairs that looked like bedrooms and had found her purse.

On the second day, they were searching her home, they found a fingerprint. Within twenty-four hours, the police had succeeded in tying the fingerprint to a name. It was difficult to analyze, but through careful comparison, the match was made. The fingerprint belonged to a forty-four-year-old Caucasian man named William Fyfe.

Chapter Four – The Man behind the Murders
William Fyfe was born in Toronto, Canada on February 27, 1955. He was later raised by an aunt for unknown reasons. While there were not any incidents during his childhood, friends later recalled there was something a little off about William. When he became an adult, he began working as a handyman.

There is little known about William's childhood as his mother was uncooperative with the police when they asked, and Fyfe spoke little about his mother and growing up. It is unclear whether negative events during his childhood caused him to become the killer he is, or if it was something else entirely.

When the police ran the fingerprint and came back with a name from Mary Glen's murder, they realized Fyfe had some previous convictions in the 1970's for breaking and entering and theft. Since then, it appeared he worked on and off as a freelance handyman, a job that gave him plenty of access to stranger's homes.

At one point, he was married and had a child, but he was with several women on and off throughout his free years. Most people called him charismatic and it was clear he got along with many. At the time the police were searching for him, his residence was Montreal, but his current whereabouts were unknown. The police struggled with the decision to put out a picture to the public naming him as a suspect because they didn't want to frighten him off, but they also wanted to protect the public.

The board decided to give the police some time before they released the photo to the public. That same day, the police received information from one of his ex-girlfriends. She suspected he was staying at his mother's home outside of Barrie, Ontario. Records were checked and it was clear he owned a vehicle, a blue Ford Ranger. This information as passed onto the Ontario provincial police, who were given the information for his potential whereabouts, as well.

Fyfe's mother lived in an old farmhouse out in the country, well off the road. It was difficult for the police to see the vehicles sitting in her driveway, but they suspected they saw a vehicle that looked similar to William Fyfe's. They backed off and waited in the area for Fyfe to make a mistake. Twenty-four-hour surveillance was set up at his mother's home to keep him from escaping and murdering another person.

Once they had him under surveillance, the police took the investigation public and released the information to the newspapers to drum up witnesses. The good thing about this is that it went national, reaching Fyfe's attention. During the surveillance, Fyfe made some key mistakes that pinpointed him as the murderer.

First, William Fyfe left his mother's home and went to Toronto where he looked for the National Post and other newspapers. Then he put in an order to the Gazette from Montreal in order to keep an eye on himself in the paper. On December 21, 1999, after three days of being home, he was in Barrie driving around. He was watched as he went to a church to drop off some running shoes outside of a bin.

The police quickly retrieved the shoes after Fyfe left the scene. The biologist confirmed spots on the shoes were blood from the victims. On December 22, 1999, the decision was made to arrest William Fyfe. The police followed him to a gas station and waited for him to appear outside. There, they arrested him for the murder of Mary Glen. As he was being arrested, he told one of the police officers:

"Why don't you shoot me now?"

Fyfe was taken to Barrie detachment and was interviewed by several officers. During the interrogation, he chain-smoked and was agitated and upset. He pulled the plug on the camera several times, was arrogant, cold, and threatened to call his lawyer, which he did several times. The police were unable to get much out of him that night, but they had his cigarette butts.

That night, the cigarette butts were sent for analysis, the shoes were sent for testing, and his mother's home and his truck were searched for evidence. On December 22nd, Fyfe was maintaining his innocence but the evidence against his was quickly mounting. The staining on his shoes was confirmed to be human, and there were more traces of blood on his clothing and in his mother's home. The three pairs of shoes he'd dropped off for donation, the hat, napkins, and many other objects were all confirmed to have human blood on them.

The investigators informed Fyfe of the evidence they had against him, and in the weeks that followed, a case against William Fyfe was created. Anna's blood was discovered on a piece of William's clothing at his mother's home. The security footage from Anna's bank showed William Fyfe in it. The bloody footprint on Monique's balcony matched one of the running shoes and the blood droplets were from Fyfe. One of Teresa's stolen rings was found amongst Fyfe's possessions. In the case of Mary Glen, the fingerprint evidence was strengthened by two more discoveries. Another bloody footprint matched the running shoes, and traces of Mary's blood was on Fyfe's clothing.

At the same time, the police were investigating all the other unsolved cases in the area for the previous twenty-five years. They received a phone call from a man named Scattolon who said he'd known Fyfe. They had played hockey together. His mother had been brutally murdered in her home and Fyfe had been inside to paint it. Scattolon wondered if there was a connection.

Almost twenty years had lapsed, yet DNA from the murdered was still available. The DNA matched William Fyfe. Hazel Scattolon was a fifty-two-year-old woman who was stabbed to death and sexually assaulted in 1981. Fyfe pled guilty on September 21, 2001, and faces twenty-five years of prison. The family members were gratified it was over and the cases were closed, but Fyfe hinted to other crimes he might have committed between 1981 and 1999.

There was a time period in the 1980's in the same areas where there was a serial rapist who raped four different women. The first woman was Suzanne Bernier, a woman who lived in Montreal and was fifty-five years old. The second woman was Nicole Raymond, a woman who lived in pointe-Claire and was twenty-six years old. The third woman was Louise Blanc, a thirty-seven-year-old resident of Ste. Adele. The fourth woman was Pauline Laplante, a forty-four-year-old resident of Piedmont.

The police believe William Fyfe was the serial rapist nicknamed The Plumber due to his method of getting into these women's homes. He would wear a plumber's uniform and claim the landlord had sent him to fix a water leak in the women's apartments. Once he was inside, he would brutally rape them.

Fyfe denied involved in Janet Kuchinksy's death. He discussed his crimes in clinical detail, letting the police know he was involved in them, but he was silent when they asked him about his motives.

William Fyfe will get out of prison when he is sixty-nine years old due to Canada having a law that allows criminals to be held for only twenty-five years. However, he has been admitted to a psychiatric hospital and chances look slim he will ever be released. Fyfe still maintains his silence on his childhood and his motives for raping and killing all these women.

If proven to be the rapist and murderer in several other open cases, he will be named Canada's worst serial killer to date. Oddly enough, Fyfe doesn't seem interested in being associated with his wrongdoings in a famous way. He seems content to remain on the sidelines, away from the spotlight, unlike most serial killers.

Conclusion

While there is a lot of media given to the cases involving serial killers, there are not that many who have either been caught or confirmed. Still, the thought of a man who seems innocent enough coming into women's homes while they are alone is enough to frighten the public into thinking about leaving their doors unlocked. Members of the communities of the victims, in this case, will never forget the women who died and how they died. William Fyfe has had an everlasting effect on the people who knew him and those who were close to his murders.

Perhaps, in time, more will be discovered about William's childhood and his motives for his crimes, but until then, we can only speculate what turned a seemingly normal child into a murderous monster.

ROBERT HOWARD

MICHAEL KAI GREEN

In October 2015, a decrepit old man named Robert Howard died of natural causes in his cell. In jail he'd led a solitary existence and spoke rarely; indeed he could have been any criminal counting down his time to release except for the fact he never stood a chance of ever getting out of prison. He was serving a life sentence for murder and simultaneously under investigation for the disappearances of other young girls that he would have had access to during a horrifically brutal life of sexual crime. Robert Howard led a gruesome life of crime, rape, brutality and murder and he called himself The Wolfman.

The name certainly conjures interesting and scary thoughts; The Wolfman sounds like a movie about werewolves or a mythical creature and he actually even gave himself a new middle name, Lesarian, believed to be a mythical child killer. He also called himself the Wolfhill Werewolf and he was certainly beastly enough to be deserving of such a name, even if he was not particularly physically grotesque.

After a criminal career that spanned 40 years, this book will look at the man behind the name, The Wolfman. I want to look at what turned him into the beast he became and why he went to such grotesque lengths with his crimes. I want to look at whether there was more to the man than meets the eye, or whether he was just a psychotic murderer and rapist. I will also look at the public opinion of him and the media interest that followed the heinous crimes committed in his active years.

MURDER FILE: ROBERT 'THE WOLFMAN' HOWARD
THE EARLY YEARS

In 1944, Robert Howard was born in an unassuming part of Southern Ireland, County Laois, in a rural area called Wolfhill. He was taller than his childhood friends and had an awkward manner, but he was bright enough and did reasonably well in his classes. Interviews with school mates at an early age suggested that had no particular disposition to some of the crimes he would go on to commit, even if he skipped compulsory school whenever an opportunity presented itself. He had 8 siblings, an uncompromising mother and his father apparently drunk a great deal of alcohol in the local pubs and taverns. When he wasn't boozing, Howard's father worked in the local brick factory and brought home barely enough for them to survive.

He was already in trouble by the young age of 13 when he was convicted of burglary and sent to a young offender's institution close to his home. Unfortunately this was not the kind of institution that troublesome kids get sent to now with emphasis on rehabilitation and morals. St Joseph's Industrial School was an institution administrated by priests and brothers and the truth about such places has only recently started to emerge. It was an Irish Catholic school and the children were starved and beaten often. Former inmates have revealed the gruelling punishments dished out by the relentless priests who would frequently humiliate the children and beat them until they bled. Names were left at the front gate and each child would be just a number, a drone whose life was often damaged irreparably by the constant beatings and starvation. Talk of sexual harassment, torture and rape has also been mentioned but never proven having been so long ago, however given the record of the Catholic Church in Ireland for covering up such instances it would not take a great stretch of the imagination to guess what might have been happening. Howard later claimed to have been a victim of such sexual abuse and used this in his defence but his crimes were ultimately indefensible. For years he would be subjected to this awful regime of farming turnips and moving rocks whilst being starved and beaten and taught the word of god.

Upon release from the institution he returned to the family home but was soon thrown out on the street by his violent, alcoholic father. Wolfhill had many abandoned coal mines leftover from its mining heyday and 16 year old Robert spent many nights sleeping rough in them. He robbed and stole to sustain himself and possibly developed a bitter and twisted view of the world on those cold, lonely nights. One young boy found that his barn had been slept in and they found a blanket and some empty cans of stolen food. They also found a journal listing criminal fantasies of how Howard wanted to break into women's houses and commit violent deeds to them. This is the first inclination we have that Howard had sexually violent fantasies and wanted to commit crimes, rather than robbing and stealing to survive.

Another local source informed reporters that he was out hunting in the woods when he stumbled upon a local farmer performing sexual acts on the young Howard. This could have been Howard's way of getting money to survive. The man did not get in the way of the pair but shot his shotgun in the air in disgust. Whether he made money by selling himself is not confirmed, although he certainly continued on a criminal spiral, stealing cars and taking goods from shops until he was caught again and sent to another, equally brutal Catholic institution. This particular precursor to prison was equally renowned as a horrific institution with beatings, humiliation and abuse rife amongst the staff and inmates. One priest would later go public in saying that it was extraordinarily violent and the boys usually ended up very disturbed.

MURDER FILE: ROBERT 'THE WOLFMAN' HOWARD
THE FIRST CONVICTED SEX ATTACKS

Presumably sick of Irish Catholic institutions, and intent on a life of crime, Howard travelled to England after release from a young offender's institution for the second time. Given the harsh conditions imposed upon him during these brutal periods it would be only logical to assume he was a fairly unstable individual at this point. He continued his life of crime in England and robbed and stole to survive, living rough whenever he could not find a place to stay.

Shortly after his 21st birthday, his crimes escalated into sexual abuse as he broke into a London home and pretended he was a doctor, ordering a young girl to undress. He attempted to rape the 6 year old girl and left violently beat her, almost killing her. He fled the scene after he heard someone coming but he escaped. Strangely, he returned to exactly the same house soon after to try again with the same girl but he got caught. His sentence seems insanely lenient as he received 9 days in borstal, and then as was common at the time, he was deported back to Ireland. The governments of both countries seemed eager to avoid media attention on keeping prisoners of the other nationality, given the troubles north of the border in Ireland, which resulted in the ridiculous 9 day sentence and subsequent deportation and release. Howard had a taste of England and chose not to stay in Ireland for long.

It seems ridiculous that a man caught red handed attempting to rape a 6 year old would have been released after 9 days in borstal, and much investigation was done into why his sentence was so lenient. Much of this centred on the political ramifications of the UK holding Irish nationals as prisoner. Needless to say, this should have been the end of the story as the Irish authorities obviously did not realise the sincerity of the situation and what heinous deeds the man they released would go on to commit.

MURDER FILE: ROBERT 'THE WOLFMAN' HOWARD CONTINUED LIFE OF CRIME

Upon his return to England, Howard was now an extremely dangerous man intent on a life of crime and sexual assault. In 1969, the same year as the Apollo moon landing, Howard found himself in Durham, and continued on his path of destruction. He broke into a house and attempted to rape a young woman, causing her immense physical injury before she escaped and ran down the road, naked and screaming in a fit of hysterics. In a fit of lustful rage he chased her but neighbours managed to get the better of him and he was promptly arrested. After a very short court session he was sentenced to 6 years imprisonment in Frankland Prison, despite the possible political ramifications. The court heard at this time of the life of crime and the judge decided that a spell in an institution was what was needed. Early release from a jail term is usually reserved for those who demonstrate good behaviour, although Howard's period in adult prison seems to have been filled with fights and bad behaviour, having assaulted a female police officer and beaten her badly before being dragged away. Despite this, or perhaps they just wanted rid of him, Howard was released from Frankland and sent back to Ireland where he did stay for a while.

Documents were much easier to forge in the 1970's and Howard had obviously gotten a false identity as he found a job in County Cork, working on a factory near the coastal town of Youghal. He called himself Lesley Cahill but although he was now employed, he would soon resume a life of crime that he had been following since a young age.

It is very easy to blame the authorities in such cases but it really looks as though something should have been done to at least attempt to evaluate and rehabilitate the Howard before he was released and allowed to go on to commit murder.

MURDER FILE: ROBERT 'THE WOLFMAN' HOWARD
THE NEXT SEX ATTACKS

Now back in Ireland, and with a new name and a new job, Howard, or Cahill as he was calling himself could have gone on to lead a somewhat normal life. It seems though, that he was intent on sexual assault and rape as a preferred career choice and before long, he was up to his old tricks. In May of 1973, Howard broke into yet another house and tried to have his way with a woman of almost 60. The house was next door to the place he'd been staying and he must have done some reconnaissance on her situation as he knew she lived alone. He stole her belongings and beta her up, breaking her ankle as e dragged her around. Her tied her to the bed and repeatedly raped her before driving away in her car. She may have died if some family did not come for a visit the following morning.

Willie Doyle, a local police officer said of the attack:

"She was a very vulnerable person. She might have suffocated, but luckily for her some relations called the next morning and found her. She was very traumatised."

After a short investigation, police concluded that Howard was the perpetrator and a warrant was put out for his arrest. He was found at Dublin airport and the police noted how passive and courteous he seemed, far too polite to be the rapist villain they were looking for. Psychologists who interviewed Howard after the arrest stated that he should have been locked up for a very long time as he was an explosive and unpredictable psychopath. He could have been sentenced to life but instead he received 10 years imprisonment. This time there would be no release for good behaviour, although by all accounts it seems his second term in a HM Prison seems uneventful. He served the majority of his sentence and was released in 1981, where upon he returned to Wolfhill in Ireland and unsurprisingly continued on his life of criminality. This time there would be fatalities, quite how many is still not known to police.

MURDER FILE: ROBERT 'THE WOLFMAN' HOWARD CONTINUED CRIMINALITY

Howard was mentioned in a report from a lady who had previous experience of sexual assault as the media found out about her appalling case of events. She was "the Kilkenny incest victim" and was repeatedly raped by her own sick father. He abused her, beat her, tortured and even impregnated her at the age of 15. She told police after the case emerged that Howard would come over to the house and drink whiskey with her father, sharing gruesome details of Howard's previous rapes and crimes and even boasting of new ones. After the story broke in the newspapers, the girl's father was arrested and sentenced to 7 years in prison. Thankfully, he would never be allowed to see his daughter again.

Somehow, Howard managed to find himself a wife and he married a young woman that he'd met in an Irish hospital. They married couple were awaiting social housing and drifted around the city of Dublin with no fixed abode for some time. Friends of the girl would have described her as vulnerable and deeply fragile, emotionally and physically, and they later told police that she'd told them just how evil and violently abusive Howard could be towards her. They lived a turbulent life together and drifted apart when he was jailed for robbery

in 1988. He served another year and a half in prison, his 3rd spell, and travelled north of the border in 1990 to check himself into an alcohol addiction facility in Newry. After the treatment, which was run by nuns and given his personal experiences with the Catholic Church can't have been too successful, he met another woman called Pat Quinn and they moved together to Castlederg in County Tyrone. They registered for public housing but had a long line in front of them and ended up in a caravan site whilst they waited. It was during this wait that another young and vulnerable woman, aged just 22 was awaiting social housing and stayed for a few nights with Howard. According to her testimony, Howard tied her up and kept her prisoner for 3 weeks whilst repeatedly raping her. Family would eventually arrive to take her away but inevitably her life would never be the same after that awful experience. The worst part of this crime was that she got pregnant as a result of the rape but did not tell police until some years later and she was considered too weak to give evidence, and so Howard was never charged with this crime.

MURDER FILE: ROBERT 'THE WOLFMAN' HOWARD PHSYCOLOGICAL PROFILING

When studied and questioned by specialists, Howard reacted very differently to what was expected. Judging from the growing list of awful crimes he had committed, psychologists expected a vile monster that was aggressive and arrogant when spoken to but he was far from that. He was smart and sophisticated, even charming when spoken to and he openly spoke of some of his crimes as though it were normal behaviour. Whether this came from his tormented life of institutions and homelessness remains to be seen but the life of crime he embarked upon sent him into a devastating spiral causing the emotional breakdown of many of his victims who were subjected to rape and vile abuse.

It was an extreme failure on the account of social services and of the authorities who failed to notice the actions and signs of a monster that was without remorse and preyed on vulnerable women of all ages and descriptions; even on children.

During sentencing for another rape charge, Dr Bownes, a psychiatrist working for the prosecution said:

"He has the propensity not only to commit further offences of a similar nature, but also to escalate his offending behaviour."

"He uses a sophisticated grooming process and selects vulnerable victims"

"Howard shows a pattern of behaviour had been established over many years and would be extremely resistant to change".

"I was somewhat surprised by the leniency of the sentence. In retrospect, we can see the system failed disastrously."

Dr Bownes was extremely concerned when the news broke about Howard's conviction and relatively short sentence of 3 years suspended sentence. Bownes had described Howard as a serial offender and if not locked away in an institution with the right facilities to treat his mental illness, he would undoubtedly reoffend and on an even larger scale.

MURDER FILE: ROBERT 'THE WOLFMAN' HOWARD THE BEGINNING OF THE END

In January of 1995, Howard, who must have been quite used to this by now, was in court on a charge of rape. Quite astonishingly, even with the psychiatric reports available, Howard was given a 3 year suspended sentence and told to stay away from younger girls. Quite what sort of message this sent to the public is beyond comprehension but Howard was released and sent home. The judge must have hung his head in shame when he heard the news to come.

Upon release Howard was almost immediately in trouble again, this time not with the law but apparently with a splinter group of the IRA. Some high ranking members found out about Howard's activities and acted to put an end to it. Howard fled to Scotland, where he informed the housing association that he was being hunted and needed a secure residence. 2 months after his suspended sentence started, Glasgow council obliged and he started to live in a rough area of Glasgow, conveniently close to schools. Pat Quinn came and stayed with him whilst he moved for unknown reasons. The ground was shrinking beneath him as the PSNI, or Police Service of Northern Ireland had got their act together and informed Glasgow council about Howard's previous actions, or the criminal record that they knew of. This alone made him the prime suspect of the murder of Arlene Atkinson. He came back and forth from Ireland, but maintained permanent residence in Scotland, and Pat Quinn left him when he found a new, vulnerable girlfriend to prey on. He met the girl in a local pub and she had a 10 year old girl, who he may have also abused at some point.

The media then started to hound him. National papers started to publish pictures of his face and list in great detail his previous convictions and possible crimes. He was linked with almost every unsolved crime in the past 30 years and the public responded violently. A mob formed and gathered at his apartment, baying for blood. Howard escaped and was moved by the police to South London, where he was similarly hounded. He moved again to different locations and social services struggled to keep up with him. In 1999, a year before the millennium, a child protection officer noted that he was living in Kent with a woman called Mary.

MURDER FILE: ROBERT 'THE WOLFMAN' HOWARD
THE END OF THE ROAD

Hannah Williams had lived an unfortunate childhood. Her parents had bitterly gone their separate ways and she herself had been subject to sexual abuse from her mother's boyfriend. She had been admitted to facilities that deal with these issues and they noted she had learning difficulties and behavioural issues. In 2001 she was living in a rundown area of Deptford, South London.

The worst possible thing then happened as she was introduced to Howard, through his girlfriend Mary as Hannah and Mary knew each other well through Hannah's mother. Howard apparently took great interest in her and the mother and Mary must have not known about Howard's past because they cannot have understood what would happen next. Hannah took a little trip to the market, alone, and met her brother who was working there. Deptford was not a particularly prosperous area and she had very little money but she dreamed of buying new clothes and shoes. Kevin, her brother remembered hearing her take a phone call and she said "I'm going now."

Hannah had never run away from home, despite her previous troubles, and her mother started to worry when she didn't come home. She had told her mother previously that she was going to meet a friend but she would never come home from wherever she was. She frantically called the police and they didn't seem to take the report seriously so Bernadette went looking on her own. She recruited friends and fellow community members who would work in shifts, driving around the streets looking for the young girl. She made posters and phoned everybody she possibly could to get any information regarding her whereabouts. Several police officers were dismissed after the investigation for not taking enough care and due diligence in the initial stages of the investigation, and with good reason. The media published her pictures and launched campaigns but she was not found and her mother was understandably heartbroken. Her body would not be found for another year.

Workers were clearing a piece of land to make way for a new flyover as part of the Channel Tunnel development when they uncovered something in the undergrowth. Almost a year after the disappearance, a machine used for clearing large pieces of dirt uncovered the decomposing body of a young girl. She had been wrapped in blue plastic and police initially thought it had been another missing girl until the matched the clothes to those Hannah had been wearing on the day she went missing. Police informed Bernadette of the discovery, but she had already seen what was going on via the news on television and she was distraught.

"I finally found out my daughter was dead, and that her body had been found, by watching it on the telly. To find out that way was unforgivable. I screamed and then I cried and cried."

"She would have made a beautiful bride, but instead of a white wedding, we had a white funeral."

Police examined the decomposing remains and did not take long to draw a list of suspects. Top of the list was Robert Howard and the giveaway had been that he'd used his girlfriend Mary's mobile phone to call her just before she died. She'd been raped and strangled in the most horrific way and the rope was still around the neck of the body when it was found. Howard was arrested in March 2002 and would not leave prison for the remainder of his life.

The trial was set for the following year and although they had no forensic evidence of Howard's involvement, they had circumstantial evidence as his whereabouts could not be proven at the time of her disappearance and the long line of character witnesses that wanted to put Howard away for the rest of his life. A young girl even came to court to tell the judge that Howard had tried to take her to exactly the same place where the murder had happened and assault her but she'd escaped.

Gradually, victims from the past bravely came forward and gave grizzly details from their ordeals at the man who called himself The Wolfman. Previous victims told of the particular methods that Howard used in his attacks, namely with the rope around the neck which happened to be the link they needed. In 3 short hours, the jury finished their verdict and were obviously sickened by the offences Howard had committed as they gave a guilty verdict and sent him for sentencing.

MURDER FILE: ROBERT 'THE WOLFMAN' HOWARD SENTENCING

The judge delivered a damning verdict of the authorities who'd let him go with lenient sentences in the past and held nothing back when delivering his verdict. Mr Justice McKinnon, the judge presiding over the case said that he had no regrets about handing Howard a life sentence and that he only wished it had been done sooner.

"It is clear that you are a danger to teenage girls and other women, and have been for a very long time."

Howard, though now serving a life sentence was also still under investigation for the murder of Arlene Atkinson, and the media were restricted on what they could publish. When the verdict of life was given, the families rejoiced as they felt they could finally start to grieve as the monster had been put away for the rest of his life. Surprisingly, Howard was acquitted of the murder of Arlene in Belfast because previous evidence could not be introduced into the court. There was a furious uproar from the public who noted the flaws of the legal system and felt Arlene deserved more justice than that. In the United States, Howard would have faced the death penalty. The jury were aware of the criminal history of Robert Howard but they were not allowed to use this as evidence.

Since the sentencing and whilst in prison, Howard cut a lonely figure and psychologists tried to study his behaviour. It seemed as though he was resigned to spending his remaining days in relative peace behind the prison walls and he kept to himself whilst the media tried to pin every crime in the unsolved case book on him. It would not surprise many to find him guilty of at least a few of those crimes and a taskforce was set up amongst investigators collaborating from Northern Ireland, Ireland and the United Kingdom. Inquiries were also set up to deal with the handling of Howard and his early releases for which there was still no explanation. He was allowed freedom when he should have had none for the earlier crimes he committed and the public were rightfully outraged.

MURDER FILE: ROBERT 'THE WOLFMAN' HOWARD
AFTERMATH

Robert Howard was the subject of much debate and media attention after the full details of his brutal past came to light. The spotlight shined on the legal system and specifically dealings and failures made between deals between the governments of the United Kingdom and Ireland. These failures let a clearly psychotic rapist loose, and allowed him to murder one girl, probably 2 and possible more.

A journalist wrote a book about missing Women from Ireland and has linked Howard to many disappearances over the periods of time he was out of jail. He stressed the importance of further investigations,

"This was a man who travelled freely all over Ireland and the UK, and lived in many places. The police should be looking at all unsolved disappearances, murders and sex crimes against women and girls during the periods when he was at large. They should be asking, 'Where was Howard?'"

As a direct result of Robert Howard, Ireland set up a sexual offenders register in 2001, many years after it should have and liaison between the police forces of all nations involved have improved when it comes to searching for dangerous suspects. The monitoring of sex offenders' on the lists in all nations involved has also improved and anonymous phone lines have been set up for victims of any sexual attacks.

The family of Hannah got closure after the trial and they would not have been sad to hear the news of his passing. His death, although he suffered in jail for some time, would have been bittersweet as young Hannah would have grown into a beautiful woman but she now would never have the opportunity. It was equally sad for the parents of Arlene Atkinson, whose parents knew the killer of their daughter, but he was never punished for the crime.

MURDER FILE: ROBERT 'THE WOLFMAN' HOWARD SUMMARY

Robert 'The Wolfman' Howard was a sick and twisted killer. He was also a skilled one that targeted vulnerable children and meticulously and ruthlessly preyed upon them. He groomed girls into thinking he was a safe person to be with and he played the system. He tracked down marginalised, vulnerable women to use as cover and seduced them into thinking he was harmless.

From a young age Howard was failed by the system. At first he was failed by the Catholic institutions for young offenders where he was beaten, starved and manipulated beyond comprehension. Only recently have these institutions been found out and closed down for good. He was also failed by his family during childhood, where he was thrown out and forced to fend for himself. The troubles in the institutions, followed by the awful upbringing and living rough meant he was not of a sound mind from an early age and the failures continued.

He was failed by the justice system of both Ireland and the UK, who failed to spot the risks he posed to the public and he was not given the correct rehabilitation and support as his crimes grew in violence and stature. In this respect the public were also failed as the justice system did not protect the scores of victims from the evil man. It was quite clear from reading the long list of crimes he committed, even before he murdered that he should not have been allowed to roam the streets as he stole and raped his way through 4 different countries. The security forces of these countries failed to keep tabs on him and monitor his life of crime.

So the life of the Wolfman would appear to be a life full of failures. He was clearly psychotic and possibly schizophrenic given the reaction of the Irish police force when the arrested him and said he seemed like a nice man. He was indeed a charming fellow, but also a brutal murderer that preyed on children and women and had a brutal past. He was of no use to anyone. Perhaps the only good thing to come from researching about this person is the fact that Ireland set up a sex offenders' list, practically as a result of his actions and support for victims of this crime grew. Liaison between police forces also developed to catch future sex attackers that try to evade the law by moving around. It does not make for good reading, researching the life of this person and not a nice a word has been mentioned about him. I feel deep sympathy for the victims' families and to the victims of his ruthless sex attacks. His was a life dedicated to crime and it was allowed to continue for a great deal longer than it should have. Let us hope that the lessons have been learned on all sides of this story and someone like Robert Howard is never allowed to do anything similar ever again.

A MONSTER IN THE CHURCH

PAULA HEARST

CHAPTER ONE

It was a cold winter night in November when the Hansen family attended a service at the Jehovah Lutheran Church in St.Paul, Minnesota. It was a "family night" at the church. Ellen Hansen and her two daughters, Cassie and Vanessa had looked forward to the evening at the church. There would be interactive games and stories plus the young girls would be able to see their friends.

Bill, the girl's father, had other business to attend to that night. He watched as his young daughters got into the car with his wife.

"It is etched in my memory," Bill Hansen recalled. "We had supper and the girls got in the car. Ellen was driving. And they were in the garage and Cassie was sitting in the passenger seat. And she (Cassie) was blowing kisses at me through the window. Waving goodbye."

Ellen arrived at the church at around 6:40 p.m for the 7:00 service. They liked to arrive early and socialize with the other church members before the sermon began. The girls proceeded to go to the children's area, located on the lower level of the church. It was their designated place to be as they usually had their Sunday School classes there, they called it the "Kid's Kingdom."

"I have to go to the bathroom," Cassie said to her mother at around 6:50 p.m.

"Okay," Ellen said. "You know where it's at?"

"I'll be right back," Cassie nodded her head.

Ellen watched her daughter leave and returned her attention to Vanessa and her other playmates. A few minutes later, however, Ellen realized that Cassie had not returned to the auditorium area and began to search for her daughter.

"Cassie?" Ellen called out.

She passed the rest of congregants milling into the auditorium. Her eyes scanning for her daughter among the clusters of families filing into the church.

"Cassie!"

"What's wrong?" one of the church staff members asked.

"I can't find my daughter," Ellen said.

The two began searching for the little girl, poking their head in the bathroom stalls and then going through every nook and cranny of the church.

"She's wearing a blue dress," Ellen said, trying to collect her thoughts. "She's blonde. Blue dress. Blue skirt. White blouse.

It started as a casual search. Cassie had probably went somewhere inside the church, got distracted and lost track of time.

"There you are!" would be the words everyone expected to hear.

As the minutes went by, however, this casual search soon turned into full blown panic. All of the staff members and congregants now began searching through the church, going upstairs and down.

"Cassie!"

Her heart pounding out of her chest, Ellen called her husband.

"I got the phone call from Ellen," Bill said. "Saying that Cassie was missing. And my heart stopped and I think I was breathing heavy, you know, just thinking 'oh boy,' because you know your child and you know that she would just not walk away from something like that. Right away, I know something was definitely wrong."

Ellen and the congregation looked throughout the church for Cassie to no avail.

The police arrived and the response was immediate. Cassie's photograph was promptly distributed to every news outlet and street flyers were made on the spot.

The search began and lasted all night.

"We stayed up all night," Ellen said. "People came all night long to help. There were a couple hundred people. Helping us search."

Police did door to door search in the neighborhood, inquiring with folks with a picture of Cassie. Church and neighborhood volunteers rallied right away and a command center was set up at the church.

There was no sign of Cassie.

She had disappeared into thin air.

CHAPTER TWO

The next morning at 11 o'clock, the police found Cassie's body

"Oh no!" one of the congregants screamed as the word was given to the people who had gathered in the church.

"The search has been called off," the officer in charge said solemnly.

In a dumpster, behind an auto repair shop that was three miles from the church, the body of Cassie Hansen had been found.

The members of the church wailed in agony. Some people stood in shock, frozen in grief.

Things like this don't happen here.

"It truly incensed the community," one of the officers on the scene said. "It incensed a lot of police officers. It was as if he seemed to be treating her as a piece of trash."

One of Cassie's leather shoes without the buckles were found a few blocks away from the dumpster while her second shoe was found later nearby.

"The idea of a church is one place you can go and you'd let your daughter go to a restroom," Catherine Lowe, crime reporter said. "That's something you would do. You'd feel a safeness, there are good people all in there together the last thing you would ever expect, and you'd have no reason to expect a stranger to come into a church and abduct a child."

The autopsy on Cassie's body would reveal no sexual penetration but that some type of sexual act had taken place.

Semen found on her dress would reveal that the perpetrator had type O blood. They would also find unusual, foreign hairs.

Cassie had been strangled to death by a two and a half inch belt, the time of death occurring between 8 o'clock and midnight. The young girl had abrasions on her body which indicated that another belt was used to restrain her. The child had been punched in her face, head, ribs and shoulder. She had scratches on her face that were consistent with someone's hand being held over her mouth.

The police did have one vague description of a possible suspect, however.

One of the church congregants reported seeing a Caucasian male, about 50-60 years old, enter the bathroom area on the night of Cassie's disappearance. He had white hair and glasses.

Who was he?

Police went to work, digging up information on any and all sex offenders in the area.

"We had a total of 107 people who had been identified by the community," an officer said. "Or through police investigation of being possible suspects. Of those 107 individuals, 57 of them either lived or worked in the area where the little girl was abducted from."

Police would rounded up these past offenders and the interrogations began.

They quickly got a suspect and then a confession.

From a crazy woman.

"Vondell Quanley," Thomas Poch said. "A woman from Texas who had claimed to have killed Cassie Hansen. And when she came to the attention of St. Paul police and allegedly made a confession it turned out that what she did was read details in the paper and then recite them. She said 'I claim I acted alone.' Well, it was quite obvious that she couldn't generate seminal fluid and that this was a sham and a fraud."

A helpful call did come in, however. Two witnesses claim that they saw an older white male carrying a motionless child near the auto body shop dumpster on the night Cassie disappeared.

Police followed up on this lead as it echoed what the church congregant witnessed near the church bathrooms.

An elderly white man. White hair. Glasses.

Needing more to go on, the St. Paul police contacted the FBI unit.

With their assistance, the FBI helped St. Paul police come up with a behavioral profile of the child murderer.

"The killer is most likely a Caucasian male," the FBI profiler said. "Someone who is considered a loner."

"How do you mean?"

"We're not talking about someone who is the life of the party here. He can blend in. He can be invisible."

"So the people in church wouldn't necessarily notice him right off the bat?"

"Precisely," the profiler said. "This is a guy who doesn't think a whole lot of himself and automatically thinks that everyone around him sees him the same way. No value. So he keeps to himself and lashes out when he can. He probably has a low-level job or is unemployed.

Probably has had numerous sex offenses in the past. He likes to frequent parks or schoolyards. You know, the creepy guy standing on the periphery. He's a voyeur. He watches his victims from afar before making his move. He trolls around at night, thinking of himself as some kind of predator. He can hide better at night. It brings out his mood, his compulsion."

"Do you think he's still here?"

"That's the illogical thing. The perp will not leave the area. He is limited in funds and can't move around easy. He feels put upon and justified in his actions. That he's entitled to whatever he wants. So he often takes a souvenir from his victims. A lock of hair. An article of clothing. Anything that marks the moment. His moment of triumph. He may also return to the scene of the crime, feeling the need to talk about it with someone."

CHAPTER THREE

The perp in the case of Cassie Hansen, did just that courtesy of Dorothy Noga.

Noga, a masseuse at the Comfort Center in St. Paul, called in a tip for the police when she became suspicious of one of her clients.

One of her customers, a cab driver named Stuart Knowlton, had been in her massage parlor the day after Cassie's murder.

Noga remembered Knowlton coming into her parlor at 3 a.m in the morning to introduce himself to the staff. He was hunched over, breathing heavy and talked really fast as if he had just been in a sprint.

He handed out business cards to everyone and received a massage from Noga.

"How's that feel?" Noga asked as she kneaded Knowlton's back.

"Great," Stuart said. "But I need a favor."

"What's that?" Noga asked, expecting the usual request for a "special" massage.

"If anyone asks, tell them I was in here last night."

That made Noga suspicious, knowing that Cassie had been murdered the night before.

Stuart Knowlton looked suspicious and fit the profile. He was Caucasian and 56 years old. Single, he worked a low-level job as a taxi driver. He had beady blue eyes set behind thick-set glasses.

Eyes that gave off the thousand yard stare that only a true psychopath can pull off.

He 'looked' the part. But was he the guy?

"I have no urge for any little girls," Knowlton said during police questioning. "I feel sorry for the little girl for her family. But I did not kill her. I didn't even know she was missing until.."

"Is it possible you killed her and forgot?"

"No sir," Knowlton said. "I did not kill her."

"Where were you on the night of the murder?"

"I was on duty driving my taxi cab. Could not have been me."

Noga followed up with police and offered to tape record her conversations with Knowlton.

Police, however, declined her offer as it would have been too dangerous for the masseuse.

The police also did not want to be seen as obtaining information illegally after Knowlton had contacted a lawyer and the lawyer had told him not to talk. Noga decided to override the police order, however. She was a good listener and could always get men to open up to her. She had four kids of her own and wanted to make the safe streets for other families.

She would then have daily phone conversations with Knowlton with same lasting deep into the night. She described him as being "lonely" and that he could not stop talking about Cassie Hansen's murder.

Noga knew that he was the man who did it.

On one occasion, Noga had taken Knowlton out for a drive. They drove past Cassie's church and noticed that Knowlton had become very agitated and wanted to leave.

The nightly phone calls soon became very taxing. Knowlton believed that the two had some kind of romantic connection. Noga was soon putting herself into a corner that she couldn't escape from.

"I would get so depressed talking to him," Noga told the St. Paul Dispatch. "I wanted to give up. I would just sit and cry."

But finally he broke.

Stuart Knowlton confessed to killing Cassie Hansen.

Noga then started taping their conversations and gave the police the tapes. The police encouraged her to keep up the conversations but Knowlton never mentioned his involvement with the murder again. He still talked about the case in a roundabout way but never confessed to the killing again.

The police would catch another break in the case as another person familiar with Knowlton came forward.

Her name was Janice Rettman. She was in charge of St. Paul's Public Housing Office and met Knowlton when he complained that he was about to be evicted from a Roosevelt Homes public housing project. He stated that his wife was leaving him and taking their two children. The welfare payments and food stamps they had been cut off and he had just begun driving a cab. Rettman investigated his claims, however, and discovered that those were not the reasons he was being evicted.

Residents had complained made sexual advances toward young girls in the housing unit.

Knowlton had let two fourteen year old girls into his apartment to play cards. Once inside, he began describing to them where babies came from and began talking about sex, birth control and menstruation. He then asked if they wanted to see his penis. The girls reported the incident to police which then informed the public housing office.

Knowlton was then given a warning by the office that if such an incident would occur again he would be evicted.

Knowlton wouldn't heed the warning. He confronted a nine year old girl and told her to take her pants off for him. The girl was so traumatized that she had recurring nightmares of Knowlton.

Knowlton's wife and children were taken to a women's shelter while he lived in an efficiency apartment. He then told Rettman of his sexual preference for children. He revealed he had spent time in a mental hospital in Traverse City, Michigan after he molested a seven year old girl. He alleged that his own father routinely beat and abused him. And he would talk about shoes a lot.

"I can't remember anyone being as chilling as he was," Rettman recalled as she knew that Knowlton frequented the area where Cassie was murdered. As a cab driver, he would be familiar with the ins and outs of the streets there, the back streets and alleys.

She would call to double-check on his housing situation and found him upset and unwilling to talk. He hung up on her but called her back a few days later. Knowlton said that he "was going through hell, was very lonely, and needed someone to talk to and to visit him."

Rettman offered her services to police, stating that she could meet with Knowlton and wear a wire.

Police accepted her offer.

Knowlton would tell Rettman about the child molestation charges from the Roosevelt Homes, his problems with his wife and his inability to hold down a job. He talked about how he converted to Christianity the previous year after being inspired by a Johnny Cash song.

Knowlton would also make reference to his "explosive temper" during their conversation and mistakenly call Rettman "Dorothy" on two occasions.

"Have you been following the news about Cassie Hansen?" Rettman asked.

"Yeah, I have," Knowlton said. "Police came and talked to me about it."

"Really?"

"They want to find out if he and I were together. If he were up there at the time of the Hansen's girls beatings. I don't even remember where I was that night."

The police then knew they had incriminating evidence against Knowlton. The fact that Cassie had been beaten up had not been released to the public.

"That was crucial and that was very critical," Thomas Poch, prosecuting attorney said. "Because no one had revealed to the press, to the media, to anyone, that she'd been beaten. And only the killer could have known that. Meanwhile, we didn't have any witnesses. It was entirely a circumstantial case."

CHAPTER FOUR

Police followed through with Knowlton's claim that he was working on the night that Cassie Hansen was murdered. With the cooperation of the taxi company, they realized that Knowlton had not turned in his log book. The log book was the time and location of all of a taxi driver's pick-ups and drop-offs.

"What happened to your log book?" police asked Knowlton in another interview.

"It was stolen," Knowlton said.

Knowlton's dispatcher, Donald Whalen would state that he tried to radio Knowlton several times during the night of Cassie's disappearance and could not reach him. Knowlton then tried to buy blank trip sheets from a competing cab company on the day Cassie's body was found.

Dorothy Noga decided to ignore police warnings that Knowlton was dangerous. With her poofy brown hair and overly applied black eye-liner, Noga did not fit the profile of a police informant. She did, however, prove to answer the hero's call when needed.

Noga called Knowlton again in the hopes of entrapping him into making incriminating statements.

"So have you been following the news about Cassie?" Noga asked. "The little girl that was murdered."

"She was a hero for us," one of the police officers said. "She told us that during one of these conversations that he admitted to her that he had killed the little girl. That he had, in effect, killed Cassie. Dorothy Noga agreed and wanted to help in the case and stated that she would be willing to talk to him and to tape these conversations. And she did this hours on end."

Knowlton, however, would not repeat what he told Noga on the phone during their earlier conversation.

Noga didn't realize how much danger she had exposed herself to. After getting off the phone with Knowlton, she was about to close her massage parlor that evening and was confronted by a man inside.

The attack was swift. She left up her hands in defense but the knife slashed through. She squirmed to get away but her assailant stabbed her in the back then slashed down her throat.

Noga crumpled to the ground, losing consciousness as she bled out.

Her assailant escaped into the darkness, blood dripping from his knife.

The thirty-two year old Noga was discovered in the parlor and rushed to the hospital.

"I proceeded to the hospital," one of the policemen on duty said. "Her throat had been slit. Her blood pressure was down to zero. They were certain she was going to die."

Noga would recover from her attack, however. She had been slashed in her throat, back and wrist right after she attempted to record Knowlton's confession.

But Noga had no recollection of the attack. She had to be placed under hypnosis in order to remember the specific details.

During hypnosis, Dorothy was able to remember who stabbed her that night.

She remembered the man's face in the darkness.

It was Stuart Knowlton.

"He jammed a knife straight on in my neck," Noga recalled in a television interview. "Then he pulled it out. Then I knew that he had cut me and I turned my head and he said 'I'll teach you not to talk' and he cut it and he slit it (her throat) all the way down."

She remembered that Stuart had confronted her and accused her of going to the police. He then confessed to the crime, giving her all of the specific details. After he confessed, he took out a knife and began chasing her around the sauna until he slashed at her throat and she lost consciousness.

CHAPTER FIVE

Minnesota State law permits testimony obtained from hypnosis, so any testimony from Noga would have been deemed inadmissible.

The police then focused on the science of the crime.

They had a semen sample that was Type O. DNA was still a long way away from acceptance back in the early 1980s but Stuart Knowlton had Type O blood. The police then acquired a hair sample from Knowlton, sending that along with Cassie Hansen's clothing to the FBI forensic laboratory.

The techs then scraped off any loose hairs and fibers from Cassie's clothing. They wanted to match Knowlton's hair sample with anything on Cassie's clothing.

"Hair comparisons are not a means of absolute personal identification," FBI Lab expert Al Robillard said. "Because a hair matches an individual or has the same microscopic characteristics as that individual's hairs, does not absolutely mean that it came from him. The reason for that is hairs are not so unique that they allow you to reach an absolute conclusion. Its possible that two hairs are so alike that they can't be distinguished microscopically could come from two separate individuals."

But Robillard would make a hair discovery on Cassie's dress that he had never seen before.

"What's so unusual in my career, looking at hairs at the FBI laboratory, I have never seen or I have never matched a hair that had this unusual characteristic. A hair disease called pili annulati. Commonly that is referred to as either ringed hair or banded hair. So I thought this was rather significant."

"If you think of looking at a racoon's tail, you actually see bands. And these bands are created because there is a breakdown in that area of the cuticle that begins to separate."

Robillard then took samples of Knowlton's hair and matched from the ones on Cassie's dress. They both had the same condition.

Pili annulati.

"No doubt about it," Robillard said looking back. "Thousands of hairs over the course of my career. I was only to put two hairs, associate a victim to a suspect, not only through the microscopic characteristics but also through a disease of the hair."

The hair was enough to arrest Knowlton for Cassie's murder.

But asthe police were closing in on Knowlton, the taxi cab driver suffered an accident.

He was crossing the street in St. Paul when a motorist ran into him. The suspect was transported to the hospital where surgeons had to amputate his left leg below the knee.

"It just seemed to me that divine intervention was there," one of the police officers said. "And that the children were going to be protected and that he would not be able to grab another child."

CHAPTER SIX

Noga would take the stand during Knowlton's trial and tell jurors of the telephone call before he attacked her.

"He said he was driving his taxi cab in the vicinity of the Jehovah Evangelical Lutheran church when he needed to use the bathroom," Noga said. "It was there I saw Cassie Hansen."

Knowlton then described greeting Cassie outside the bathroom, talking to her about the church services.

"Would you like to play a game?" he asked.

The girl nodded but remained unsure.

Knowlton lured her outside. Cassie began to cry.

He then her into his cab and molested her.

The little girl kept crying so he put his hand over her mouth until she stopped breathing.

He would then take off both of her shoes before placing her into the dumpster. Knowlton had removed the buckle from the shoe and kept it as a souvenir before dumping the shoes in two separate locations.

"Stuart had a shoe fetish," Janice Rettman said. "When he talked about shoes at first, it meant nothing to me. In retrospect, it was probably more significant than I thought."

The unique hair found on Cassie's hair clothing that matched Stuart Knowlton's own hair strand was enough to convince the jury to find him guilty of first degree murder and second degree misconduct.

He was sentenced to life in prison.

"The evidence from the FBI laboratory was absolutely critical and one piece of evidence that was absolutely essential to tying him in and being able to get a conviction of Stuart Knowlton."

Knowlton was given an opportunity to speak after his sentencing and he went on an incoherent ten minute rant.

"As God is my witness," Knowlton rambled on "I swear to you this day, I did not abduct Cassandra Lynn Hansen from the church she was attending. I had no reason to take anyone's life for God had not given me that right. I have had no reason to have any vengeance against Cassandra Lynn Hansen or Dorothy Noga."

Knowlton would die in prison in 2006 after being denied parole in 2001.

After his sentencing, the Hansen family started a foundation called "Save Cassie's Friends." Two hundred books were printed out in Cassie's honor, raising awareness of child abduction.

SERIAL KILLER GRANDPARENTS : THE TRUE STORY OF RAY & FAYE COPELAND

OLIVIA WATSON

Chapter One

Ray and Faye Copeland are often known as the oldest couple ever to be sentenced to death in the United States. At the ages of 76 and 69, the couple was sentenced to death in separate trials for the murders of five vagrant men that they had taken in, hired, forced to commit fraud, and then finally killed to keep quiet.

While Ray's guilt in the crime was indisputable, Faye's role in the crimes is muddled as she was the victim of severe physical abuse at the hands of Ray. Was she truly involved in the crime? Or was she simply a victim herself?

Ray Copeland was born in Oklahoma in 1914. He had a tough childhood—his family was struggling to survive the Depression and moved around a lot. To help support his family, Ray began a life of petty crime as a young man. He would forge cheques and steal livestock every chance he could.

In the late 1930's, this life of crime caught up to Copeland and he was arrested and sentenced to a year-long jail sentence. After his release in 1940, he met Faye Wilson, a young woman who belonged to a simple family. The two connected and Ray won Faye's heart by promising to always protecting her.

Ray and Faye married only a few months after first meeting. They decided to move from Oklahoma to Missouri and Ray quickly found them a property on the outskirts of the small town of Mooresville. The property was a small plot of farmland that had a simple farmhouse and a few barns, but lots of space for bringing up cattle.

Ray had spent his whole life taking care of cattle, and was convinced that raising and selling cattle would be his fast track path to building a proper life for himself and his family. Ray and Faye had several children in quick succession, which meant that they needed money fast. It wouldn't be long until Ray returned to his old ways, and began to use crime as a means for obtaining money.

Chapter Two

In the late 1980's cattle auction houses throughout the state of Missouri were frequently being swindled. Buyers would show up, make their purchase, pay by cheque and then disappear. The cheques were inevitably worthless.

To combat this problem, cattle auctions in the area began to keep track of buyers who were known to not be good for their money, and they shared these names with other cattle auction houses. If you were blacklisted by one auction house, you would be blacklisted at all the others in the area as well.

Ray Copeland quickly made it onto the cattle auction blacklists. After returning to a life of crime, he quickly built up an increasingly bad reputation. This caused a lot of problems—his whole livelihood was raising cattle and now he couldn't purchase any cattle to raise unless he paid in cold hard cash, something he didn't often have.

Faced with the realization that he could no longer buy cattle himself, he lacked the means to move his family to a new area, and that he was tired of wasting time in jail, he came up with a new plan: a way to use his illegal money-making methods that would allow him to remain undetected.

Ray Copeland began to hire vagrant men from the area to go to cattle auctions with him. He would have the men bid and pay for cattle using his own bad cheques and then sell the cattle before the auction houses realized the cheques bounced. This way, if the auction houses came after someone in relation to the bad cheques, the vagrant men would be responsible, not Ray Copeland.

This scheme worked for Copeland for quite a while. It confused a lot of auction houses and the local police forces for quite some time. As Leland O'Dell, a former sheriff from rural Missouri explained: "It was so odd that so many of them would have cheques but when we went to go look for them, we couldn't find them. We would enter them into the computer, but they never showed up."

Copeland's scheme was smart. No one would expect a man with cheques to be vagrants, and most vagrant men were incredibly difficult to track down.

Eventually, this scheme caught up to Copeland. After police were able to find and interview some of the vagrant men they found out that they had almost all been hired by Ray Copeland. Ray was arrested for his involvement and spent his later incarceration determining how he could further improve this plot.

A while after Ray had been released from jail, the instances of successful cattle fraud scams occurring began to rise again. This time though, all the buyers were repeat customers of the auction houses and none of them could be traced down to be questioned. The only thing that connected them was that at some point in time, many of the buyers had all worked on the same farm owned by 78-year-old Ray Copeland and his wife Faye.

But who exactly were Ray and Faye Copeland, and why had so many of their previous employees seemingly disappeared without a trace?

The answer to this would shock police and Missouri's rural community to their very cores.

Chapter Three

To most, the Copeland's were a regular family living a simple life on their small farm. They appeared to be just a regular elderly farm couple that was a bit shy. They didn't like to socialize with a lot of other people, but that was never really a problem. They seemed completely ordinary.

The Copelands had a difficult life though. Their small farm wasn't enough to support the family so Faye took jobs in local factories and worked as a maid in local motels. When asked why she stood with her husband through all of this difficulty, Faye Copeland simply answered, "Because he was my husband. I was taught from childhood that when you married someone, you stayed with them. The husband was the boss. Ray was always the boss."

The whole family, including Faye, also was required to help out on the farm. They were in way over their heads with the amount of chores and work that needed to be completed everyday, even though none of them earned the family any extra money. Faye would wake up early to go muck out cattle stalls before work.

The family was so poor that when Faye did this, she did it barefoot despite the season. She had one pair of shoes and didn't want them destroyed. She needed them clean to keep up appearances while she spent the rest of her day working her other jobs in town.

When the Copeland children left the farm, Ray looked for farmhands. He was up in age, deaf, and not a great businessman. He was also illiterate. He couldn't read or write which made it difficult for him to keep track of how the business was going. He needed someone to help out with the chores, but also the business side of the ever-struggling farm.

To find these workers, Ray would visit local homeless missions. He would come in and ask people if they would like to go out and make some money and get paid at the end of the day. He would even offer to help the men get set up with bank accounts for their new finances.

These men were almost always vagrants. They were men who were usually on the run, they had addictions, family problems, and mental illness. Most had been arrested for vagrancy or petty theft. Ray Copeland would pay them $50 a day for their labour and would provide them with room and board if the workers wanted to stay on at the farm long-term. For someone who had been previously homeless, a steady paycheque and a place to live in a quiet rural setting would have been paradise. Many jumped at Ray Copeland's offer.

One of the men who went to live and work on the Copeland's farm was 27-year-old Dennis Murphy. Murphy was a drifter from Illinois who was down on his luck when Copeland offered him steady work and a place to live. Murphy was also wanted in connection to writing bad cheques to cattle auction houses.

In 1986, a sheriff's deputy following up on Murphy's several instances of fraud visited the Copeland farm after hearing from other vagrant men that he had gone there to work and hadn't been seen since. The deputy asked Copeland if he knew Murphy's recent whereabouts. Copeland replied that the man had simply took off one day, and he hadn't heard from him since.

Copeland claimed that most of the workers he hired would leave in the middle of the night and he would never see them again. Murphy was only one example of this. When Copeland was told that Murphy was a thief, he said he wasn't surprised. He had been swindled too. Copeland also had a cheque from Murphy that had bounced due to insufficient funds.

Unbeknownst to Ray Copeland, seven other men in addition to Murphy were currently being investigated in connection to local cattle auction scams. The police had been having an incredibly difficult time tracking down any of the eight men and were getting close to determining that all eight must have left town immediately after committing their crimes.

One day however, a call from an unlikely informant in Nebraska opened up a whole new path of investigation for the police—a path with a sinister turn. What if none of the men could be found because after committing their own crimes, they all became the victim of a heinous serial killer.

Chapter Four

The unlikely informant from Nebraska was Jack McCormick, a drifter and small time conman who had at one time worked on Ray Copeland's farm. He liked to tell stories and told police that he thought he had seen human remains including a skull on the Copeland's farm during his time there.

Due to the extensive criminal past Copeland had, and the fact that many of the missing men had worked for Copeland as well, police decided to follow up on McCormick's story.

The Copeland's farm covered 40 acres and included a pond, a barn, fields, and woods. A major search was launched on the property by police. They surveyed the area looking for possible burial sites, human remains, or crime scenes. Scent dogs and backhoes were both used in the search which lasted for weeks. Searchers even poked holes in the walls to find any hollow hiding spots.

After nine days of searching without success, police began to doubt McCormick's story so they decided to bring him back to his former employers farm.

Former sheriff O'Dell was one of them men who brought McCormick back to the Copeland's farm. He remembers telling the man just point to where this skull and leg bones were.

When confronted with this, McCormick got nervous. He told police he could've been mistaken. Perhaps he had actually just seen a discarded pan or other large object poking the bushes. He asked to be taken away from the farm right away—he didn't want to spend a minute more than needed to there.

After this frustrating experience, police decided to launch an in-depth investigation into the background of Ray Copeland. What they found showed an interesting coincidence. Twenty years earlier, Copeland had been arrested several times for the same thing his vagrant workers had—writing bad cheques.

Copeland had seemingly calmed down since then, though. It had been over 20 years since he had wound up in jail, and he had never been arrested for a violent crime. Police soon learned that Copeland worked on some other farms in the area to earn extra money.

One such farm was only a few miles from Copeland's own farm. These properties now needed to be searched as well. Although they weren't quite sure how all the pieces fit together yet, police were almost certain that the disappearance of Murphy and the seven other missing vagrant men were somehow connected to Copeland.

When police searched this secondary location, they made a startling discovery in the barn were Copeland worked moving around large bales of hay. In the back corner of the barn, hidden underneath and behind several large hay bales was a shallow grave—in it, were the bodies of three men lined up head-to-toe-to-head. They had probably been in the grave for two or three years, and were now completely unrecognizable due to the amount of decomposition that had taken place.

The bodies were wrapped in blankets, which kept them dry so they had not decomposed down to skeletal remains. To help this, the soil was also clay, which helps to ward of decomposition as well. Instead, the skin of the bodies had dried out and shrivelled like a mummy.

The three men had been killed by single gunshot wounds to the head. But there was no evidence linking Ray Copeland or anyone else to the crimes. A few days later in another barn on the same property police removed hundreds of bales of hay and found another body under a floorboard.

Six weeks later in a nearby well was yet another body. This man had been wearing a belt that read Dennis across the front. But was this Dennis Murphy? And was his killer Ray Copeland?

Chapter Five

After police found the remains of five different men on a farm connected to Ray Copeland, they reinterviewed McCormick. This time, McCormick was more confident in his memories of his former boss.

McCormick told police that Ray Copeland had been running a cheque fraud scam. He said Copeland had given him a few hundred dollars to open a chequing account and told him to list a post office box as his address. He then took McCormick to cattle auctions and sat in the stands, signalling to McCormick when to bid on the cattle.

When he won the bidding, McCormick would pay for the cattle with a cheque. After a couple of his cheques cleared he would be in good standing with the auction house. They next time they returned, he was able to spend more money and write even larger cheques under the pretence that the cheque would be good as well when it was brought to the bank. It almost always bounced the second time.

Copeland would sell the cattle bought under McCormick's name and kept the profits himself. But before the cheque had a chance to bounce, Copeland confronted McCormick with a gun.

Copeland told McCormick that there was a raccoon living in a hole in his barn and he needed the worker's help to get rid of it. He wanted McCormick to crouch down next to the hole and poke the raccoon with a stick while Ray waited with his gun. At this time, McCormick was already nervous around his large, aggressive boss who he knew was orchestrating a fraud scam at the time.

The skittish McCormick bent to Copeland's will and began to crouch down in the barn and poke at the hole with a stick. When nothing happened, Ray told him to keep going. McCormick felt a chill go up his spine and quickly looked back up at his boss to see him pointing his '22 rifle not at the hole where the raccoon was allegedly going to be running out of but directly at his own head.

McCormick promised Ray he would leave the area and never come back if he spared his life. Ray agreed, and McCormick immediately left Missouri behind him. For five months the vagrant man was quiet about his ordeal, and Ray's scam plot, as he still feared Copeland. He knew his former boss had no problems taking lives, so he did what he felt he needed to do to protect his.

When Police searched the Copeland's home, they found a '22 rifle and an assortment of men's clothing, none of which belonged to Ray. They also found several pairs of men's shoes in a range of sizes, none of which fit Ray or their sons, and a bunch of empty suitcases.

Most damningly though, hidden in a camera case was a list of names. The list was a record of men who had worked for Ray Copeland in the past. Next to four of the names was an X, which corresponded with four vagrant men who were wanted in connection to bad cheques that had been given to pay for cattle at nearby auctions. One of which, was Dennis Murphy.

Four names were marked with an X on Copeland's list, and five bodies had been found hidden around a farm Copeland had worked on. It was obvious to investigators that they needed to find a way to have the four bodies positively identified as soon as possible.

Chapter Six

Investigators working on the Copeland case sent the skulls of the five bodies to a forensic odontologist who photographed and x-rayed each of the skulls to compare the dental markings to dental charts from each of the men whose names had been marked with an X. Although this is a common practice in the world of forensic science and criminal investigation, this instance proved difficult.

All the men on Copeland's list were vagrant and homeless. While they all had dental records on file from their childhoods, they were now extremely out-of-date. None of the men had received recent dental care. Without recent records, and with a lifetime worth of damage due to improper care, it was difficult to determine whether the dental records didn't match the skulls because they weren't the same people, or if they didn't match any more because of the outdated records.

One of the skulls, however, was easily matched to previous records because of irregularities in the bones around the teeth. This skull had been from the body found in the well on the farm, and it was positively identified as being Dennis Murphy.

Eventually, the four other skulls were able to be positively identified. Three of the four had been names marked with an X on Ray Copeland's list.

The five bodies were sent to Coroner Scott Lindley to be autopsied. In each case, the cause of death was found to be from gunshots fired from a close distance.

"If the shot is fired from close range, the inside of the skull tends to break or flake away and there is more small fractures and damage done to the skull altogether," Lindley has explained.

Inside each of the skulls Lindley also found bullets and bullet fragments. Markings on the bullets were later conclusively determined to have been able to come from only one gun—Ray Copeland's '22 caliber rifle.

Faced with this information, police confidently arrested Ray Copeland for the five men's murders. In a move that shocked many, they also arrested Ray's wife Faye, who they believed had been his accomplice.

But what role exactly did 68-year-old Faye Copeland play in the murders?

Chapter Seven

Faye Copeland claimed she knew nothing about Ray's crimes. She knew about his previous convictions for fraud, of course, but had no idea that Ray had been murdering their employees in a more modern cattle fraud scheme. According to Faye, when the workers disappeared Ray told her that they had simply run off or that he had fired them and they left right away. She had no reason to doubt her husband's stories, the men were vagrants after all, and Ray had emotionally and physically abused Faye their entire marriage so she wasn't about to question him for details.

While in prison, Faye wrote a letter to her husband assuring him that things would calm down soon. While it was meant to be a calming gesture to the man she was married to, Faye's letter was taken by police and used as a known handwriting sample to be compared to the list of names found in the Copeland's home. Faye's handwriting matched the list of the missing men.

While police saw this as damning evidence Faye maintained her insistence that she had no idea about the murders. She explained to police that Ray was illiterate so he often got her to write lists and notes for him all the time. She never asked any questions, it wouldn't have done her any good. When Ray felt like she was questioning his thoughts or choices he simply slapped her across the house to get her to stop.

No one outside of the family had any indication that Ray may have been abusing his wife, but Ray and Faye's children could recall thousands of times Ray lost his temper and took it out on his wife or his children. Al Copeland, one of Ray and Faye's sons, once recalled to police a time when Ray smacked Al's younger brother with a frying pan because he had been scraping the last few mouthfuls of oatmeal out of his bowl with a spoon and Ray didn't like the noise.

Violence had been an everyday occurrence in the Copeland household.

Ray and Faye Copeland were tried in court separately. Prosecutors believed that Ray had acted alone in orchestrating the fraud schemes, including murdering the men afterwards to keep them quiet, but that Faye had known what was going on the whole time, which would make her criminally responsible as well.

There was no questioning Ray's guilt in court. Investigators were able to prove that each of the five men had died at the other end of Ray's gun after being lured to work for the man and then used as pawns in a cattle fraud scheme. It was irrefutable evidence.

Ray was quickly found guilty on all five counts of murder and other related charges including fraud. He was sentenced to death by lethal injection. Even his own children celebrated Ray's death sentence, viewing it as justice served for the horrible way he treated everyone around him, and for the horrible acts he committed simply to make extra money without having to do extra work.

Throughout her trial, Faye continued to claim she had no involvement and no knowledge in Ray's actions—he had committed his crimes all by himself. Faye was simply an abused wife her put her head down and did what she was told to do. Throughout her life she had carried bruises and broken bones for nothing and had spent most of her life doing everything possible to avoid Ray's violence. Her greatest crime was not asking questions.

The list of workers in Faye Copeland's handwriting, however, sealed her fate. It was the smoking gun of the prosecutor's case, and it got Faye convicted for all five murders as well. She also received a sentence of death.

Before Ray Copeland could be executed he died in prison in 1993. Six years later, in 1999 Faye's attorneys appealed her conviction on the basis that Faye had been too terrified of her former husband to admit her life long abuse at his hands. The abuse had been the reason Faye had written the list, but jurors had never heard this before. The only previous explanation previously could have been that she was involved.

On this basis, the courts commuted her death sentence to life in prison, but her convictions remained. Three years later, Faye suffered a stroke which left her partially paralyzed and unable to speak. She was released from prison a week later on medical parole, fulfilling her final wish not to die in prison. Faye passed away from natural causes less than a year later on December 23, 2003.

BONUS:

Franklin Delano Floyd

Franklin Delano Floyd's life was a long series of strange and tragic occurrences, beginning with the death of his father when Floyd was just a year old. Floyd grew up in an orphanage and turned to a life of crime at a young age, earning himself a lengthy criminal record over his lifetime. By the age of 20, in the year 1963, he was imprisoned for the kidnapping and rape of a 4 year old girl. He escaped from prison, robbed a bank, and then served a ten year prison term.

Floyd was released on parole and soon after committed another crime, attempting to kidnap a woman. He was arrested but posted bail quickly. Floyd then disappeared, spending much of the rest of his life on the run from authorities and using false names to hide his true identity.

However, Floyd's string of disturbing and violent crimes didn't stop. Around the time he disappeared, in 1974, Floyd married a woman in North Carolina. Floyd kidnapped two of the woman's children, including her five year old daughter, Suzanne Sevakis, who came to be known as Sharon Marshall. Floyd raised Marshall as a daughter, though later evidence showed he molested her from a young age. The two moved frequently around the country and used aliases to conceal Floyd's identity.

In the late 1980's, Marshall graduated from high school. A few years later she gave birth to a son named Michael Hughes, who it was later determined was not Floyd's biological son. Soon after, Marshall began working as an exotic dancer. It was during this time, in April of 1989, that Floyd committed the murder of Cheryl Commesso, a fellow dancer at the club where Marshall worked.

Commesso's murder went unsolved for years. Later in 1989, Floyd and Marshall were married. But in 1990, Marshall was killed in a hit and run accident. The driver was never found, and Floyd remains the only suspect in the case to this day. Later that year, Floyd was arrested for the kidnapping he committed in 1973.

Floyd again served a short prison sentence and was released in 1993. But Floyd didn't stop his life of crime. Shortly after serving his time in prison, Floyd attacked another woman. He was arrested for this attack but released on bond. During this time, Floyd went to the elementary school of Michael Hughes, Marshall's son, who had been living with a foster family. He kidnapped Hughes and the school principal, leaving the principal tied to a tree in the woods. The principal was found and survived, but Hughes was never found.

Floyd was finally arrested again in 1994 for the kidnapping of Hughes, though this would be the last time he was incarcerated. In 1995, Commesso's remains were found. The same year, a truck that had belonged to Floyd was found to contain images of child pornography along with pictures of Commesso severely beaten. This evidence was used to convict Floyd of Commesso's murder. In 2002, Floyd was sentenced to death for the murder of Cheryl Commesso and the kidnapping of Michael Hughes.

Early Life

From a very young age, Franklin Delano Floyd led a troubled life. He was born on June 17, 1943 to Thomas H. Floyd and Della Jewel Floyd in the town of Barnsville, Georgia. He had four siblings—a brother Billy and three sisters, Dorothy, Shirley, and Tommye.

In June 1944, when Floyd was just one year old, his father passed away. This left Floyd and his four siblings in the care of his mother, an unstable woman who would go on to have several failed marriages and her own criminal record. In January of 1946, the young Floyd and his siblings were placed in the Georgia Baptist Children's Home by their mother. Floyd's sister Dorothy was later separated from the others and moved to another orphanage in Pinewood, Georgia.

Floyd's mother moved to Florida where she married and subsequently divorced twice. She then married her fourth husband, who she would stay with for the rest of her life. It is unlikely that Floyd ever saw his mother again, though she did visit his sister Dorothy once, a trip that ended with Della being arrested on a drunk and disorderly charge.

In the summer of 1959, when he turned sixteen, Floyd ran away from the children's home he had been living in since he was just two years old. Shortly after running away, Floyd obtained falsified documents claiming he was eighteen years old. He used these papers to join the U.S. Army, using his real name but a fake age.

Floyd's Army career was short-lived, however. He was stationed in Missouri and Oklahoma before his real age was discovered in December of 1959. Upon discovering he was only sixteen, the Army sent Floyd via bus to his sister Dorothy. Dorothy had married since leaving the orphanage and now lived in Gainesville, Georgia. When Floyd arrived, however, Dorothy's husband did not allow him to stay.

A few months later, Floyd began what would ultimately be a life of crime. Early in the morning on February 19, 1960, Floyd broke into a Sears store in Inglewood, California. Police arrived at the scene and Floyd exchanged fire with the police on the roof of the building. He was shot in the back and hospitalized for his injuries at Centinela Hospital.

After recovering somewhat, Floyd was transferred to the prison ward in nearby General Hospital before being sent to the Preston Youth Correctional Facility. His sentence was not long, and by the summer of 1961 Floyd was out on parole. However, in August of 1961 he violated his parole by leaving the country and going on a camping trip in Canada. Floyd was arrested in November of 1961 for this parole violation and was returned to the Preston Youth facility.

A few months later, in January of 1962, Floyd was released. He left California, returning to his home state of Georgia where he briefly lived with his sister Dorothy in Gainesville. He then moved nearer to Atlanta, where Floyd worked at the Atlanta airport for a short period of time. In May of 1962, Floyd moved back to Hapeville, Georgia and lived near the Georgia Baptist Children's Home where he grew up. It was during this time that Floyd, now nineteen years old, began to commit more horrific crimes.

Kidnapping and Bank Robbery

On May 20, 1962, Floyd kidnapped a four year old girl from a bowling alley in Hapeville, Georgia. Floyd subsequently raped the girl. On July 31, 1962 he was found guilty of child molestation and was sentenced to 20 years in prison. However, Floyd would never serve his full sentence for this crime.

Floyd was sent to Reidsville Prison in Atlanta, Georgia to serve his time. In November of 1962 he was hospitalized at Milledgeville Hospital where he underwent psychiatric testing. Floyd had a number of psychiatric problems, possibly stemming from his difficult childhood spent in an orphanage. His stay at the hospital was lengthy, spanning more than four months.

On March 14, 1963 Floyd escaped from Milledgeville Hospital. Outside the hospital, he stole a car and purchased a pellet pistol. Floyd used these to commit a bank robbery, later claiming he needed to get money to appeal his child molestation conviction. He stole over $6,800 from the Citizens and Southern Bank in Macon, Georgia, and was caught and arrested the same day. Floyd soon confessed to the crime.

On July 12, 1963, Floyd was sentenced to fifteen years in prison for the bank robbery. He was sent to Chillicothe Federal prison in Chillicothe, Ohio. Floyd remained there for several months, though in September of 1963 he attempted to escape by hotwiring a prison fire truck and crashing it into a fence. The escape attempt was unsuccessful.

In October, Floyd was transferred to a prison in Lewisburg, Pennsylvania where he remained until June of 1964, when he was sent to a prison hospital in Springfield, Missouri to be evaluated. Floyd stayed in the hospital for eight months before being transferred to a federal prison in Marion, Illinois.

The prison in Marion was Floyd's longest stay in one facility to that point, and he remained there from February of 1965 until February of 1968. During this time he earned his GED. Floyd's mother also passed away while he was in prison in Marion. In February 1968 Floyd was again transferred, this time back to Reidsville, Georgia. He finished his sentence for child molestation there.

In November 1971, Floyd was sent to a federal prison in Atlanta, Georgia to serve his sentence for his escape attempt in Chillicothe. He was there for another year, and in November 1972, Floyd was released to a halfway house. Soon after, on January 19, 1973 he was paroled.

Just over a week later, on January 27, 1973, Floyd attempted to kidnap a young woman. On February 2nd, he was arrested for the attack. Floyd called a friend he met during his time in prison who bailed him out. After this incident, Floyd disappeared for several years, becoming a fugitive on the run.

Sharon Marshall

Sometime between 1973 and 1975, Franklin Delano Floyd, using an alias, married a North Carolina woman by the name of Sandra Chipman. Chipman had four children, including a baby boy, a five year old girl, and two other daughters. In 1974, Chipman was arrested and served 30 days in jail for writing bad checks. While she was in jail, Floyd took two of her children—the baby boy and the five year old girl—and fled the state. The other two children were placed in a children's home.

When Chipman was released from jail, she was able to reunite with the two children Floyd had left behind. However, Floyd and her other two children were long gone. Chipman attempted to file a report with the police, but she was told that because Floyd was the children's stepfather he had the right to take them.

Chipman's infant son was never seen again, and his whereabouts remain unknown to this day. Her young daughter Suzanne Sevakis, however, remained with Floyd. He gave her several different aliases during her childhood, as he was still a fugitive, but as she grew older the girl went by the name of Sharon Marshall.

In 1975, Floyd got a job working for the Oklahoma school system. In August of 1975, he enrolled Marshall at Wilson Elementary School in Oklahoma. Floyd went by the false name of Trenton Davis while Marshall was enrolled in school as his daughter under the name Suzanne Davis.

In 1978, Floyd had to move again. A babysitter told police that she believed Floyd, or Trenton Davis, was molesting his "daughter". Floyd appeared again in Arizona briefly, where Marshall was again enrolled in school. They didn't stay long, moving to Louisville, Kentucky in 1979.

In 1983, Sharon Marshall began high school. She attended three different schools in 1983 as Floyd moved around, taking her with him. Floyd finally settled in Atlanta, Georgia, assuming the name Warren Marshall. Sharon Marshall enrolled in Forest Park High School, where she was a surprisingly successful student.

Marshall was a smart girl and a good student. By the time she graduated, she had even earned college scholarships for her academic excellence. Not just smart, Marshall was also a popular student. She ran for junior class office and, according to her teachers, was well-liked. She attended a student council leadership conference one summer, where she befriended Jennifer Tanner.

Tanner was later able to give accounts of her friendship with Marshall, shedding light onto Marshall's mysterious life. According to Tanner, Marshall's "father", Floyd, was very strict. She also stated later that Marshall showed her lingerie Floyd had given her. Adding to the strangeness of their relationship, Tanner also said that Floyd was obsessive about Marshall's looks, frequently taking photographs of the teenager.

In 1986, Sharon Marshall graduated high school. She had done well enough to earn a full scholarship to go to Georgia Tech and study aerospace engineering. However, she never went to college and instead stayed with Floyd. Marshall moved to Phoenix, Arizona with Floyd in July 1986. In 1988, Marshall got pregnant. She attempted to run away to Alabama to be with her boyfriend, but he woke up to find her missing one day. She left behind a note saying her father had taken her back with him. Marshall was back with Franklin Delano Floyd.

On March 21, 1988 Marshall gave birth to a baby boy and named him Michael Anthony Hughes. Even after Hughes's birth, Marshall and Floyd continued to move around frequently.

By April of 1989, Marshall and Floyd were living in Tampa, Florida. Marshall was working as an exotic dancer at the Mons Venus club. This is where they met Cheryl Commesso, the woman Floyd was ultimately sentenced to death for killing.

Cheryl Commesso

Cheryl Commesso was a native of the Tampa, Florida area. Just a few years younger than Marshall, she had attended the local Brandon High School, where she participated in extracurricular activities, including singing in the chorus and dancing. Commesso even competed in the Miss Brandon pageant in 1987. Commesso, according to surviving family members, was a bright young girl who just grew up too fast.

In her senior year of high school, Commesso began to run away. She dropped out of school and began dancing at the World Famous Doll House a strip club in Orlando, Florida. Commesso was living fast—she bought a red Corvette and earned enough money dancing to get breast implants. According to her mother, Lois Commesso, she wanted to model for Playboy someday.

In 1989, Commesso was working at the Mons Venus near Tampa, Florida, where she lived with her father. She met and befriended Sharon Marshall who was also working as a dancer at the club.

The friendship turned into a deadly mistake for Commesso. In late March of April 1989, shortly after St. Patrick's Day, Commesso and Marshall got into an argument outside the Mons Venus club. Floyd became involved, accusing Commesso of reporting Marshall for falsely reporting her income, which had resulted in Marshall losing Medicaid coverage for her infant son. According to a coworker of Commesso and Marshall's, Floyd punched Commesso during this argument, leaving a bruise.

Not long after the altercation, Commesso went missing. It was later discovered that Floyd, possibly with Marshall's help, had kidnapped Commesso. Nobody knows exactly where he took her or all the graphic details of what he did to her, but Floyd did leave some clues, whether he meant to or not.

Commesso was last seen by her family a few days before the murder. She was leaving for several days. Commesso packed a bag and told her father she would call him soon, then left, never to be seen alive again. Her car was soon found in the parking lot of the St. Petersburg/Clearwater airport. This immediately aroused suspicions in her family, who told police that Commesso was very attached to her car and would never have left it.

Commesso's fate remained unknown for years. Finally, in 1995, landscapers found her skeletal remains in a wooded area off of Interstate 275. Medical investigators determined the woman whose skeleton they found, known at the time as "Jane Doe I-25", had been beaten and shot in the back of the head twice. They were also able to identify the body as Commesso's, with evidence suggesting the body had been there for six to seven years, the same amount of time as Commesso had been missing.

Back on the Run

Floyd's other criminal enterprises did not stop during this time. In April of 1989, the very same month that Commesso was murdered, a warrant was placed on Floyd for insurance fraud. Floyd was accused of drilling holes into the bottom of a boat he owned in order to collect insurance money.

Floyd and Marshall were also the primary suspects in Commesso's mysterious disappearance, thanks to the altercation coworkers had witnessed between Floyd and Commesso shortly before she disappeared. Floyd left town soon after murdering Commesso and brought Marshall along with him. The pair left Tampa, Florida in May of 1989 and moved to New Orleans. On June 15, 1989, Floyd and Marshall married, with both the bride and groom using new aliases.

The very next day, June 16, 1989, Floyd's trailer in Tampa burned to the ground. Police ruled that this was intentional arson. Most likely, Floyd was attempting to hide the evidence of Commesso's murder as well as his own identity, as he was still wanted for the 1973 kidnapping case in Atlanta. It appeared that, at least for the moment, Floyd was going to keep running from the law.

Soon after these events, Floyd and Marshall moved again, this time to Tulsa, Oklahoma. In August of 1989, Marshall began working at another adult entertainment nightclub called Passion. She and Floyd would live together in Oklahoma for several months with Marshall working as a dancer. Coworkers say that Marshall was secretive about her past, telling them only that all members of her family were dead.

During her time at Passions, Marshall also confided in some of her coworkers, though she never revealed the truth about her life. She did, however, tell coworkers that she had a new boyfriend whom she had met at the club. Marshall's coworkers claim she was afraid to tell her husband that she wanted to leave him.

Marshall was right to fear what Floyd might do. Less than a year after their marriage in New Orleans, Marshall was killed in a mysterious hit-and-run accident.

Hit-and-Run

On the night of April 25, 1990, the woman who had come to be known as Sharon Marshall was struck by a car while walking on the side of the road to the motel where she was staying in Tulsa. Marshall was hospitalized and survived for five days with her injuries before dying on

April 30, 1990. Her funeral was held in Tulsa, Oklahoma on May 4, 1990.

Floyd was a person of interest in the case. He claimed that he was in the motel waiting for her and therefore could not have been the driver in the hit-and-run accident. Floyd was not arrested, though police had their suspicions.

On May 17, 1990, less than two weeks after his mother's death Michael Hughes, Marshall's son, was declared a ward of the state. Hughes was placed in foster care. According to his foster parents, Hughes, who was two years old, was non-verbal and had limited muscle control. His behavior was frequently out of control. Nevertheless, Hughes began to make progress during his time with his foster family.

Identity Revealed

On June 20, 1990, Floyd was finally caught and his true identity as Franklin Delano Floyd was revealed. He was arrested near Augusta, Georgia where he had been living in a trailer, for the 1973 kidnapping attempt he had committed in Atlanta. Floyd was sent to a federal prison in Georgia, and in December of 1990 he was transferred to El Reno Prison in Oklahoma.

Floyd spent a total of 33 months in El Reno Prison. During this time, Michael Hughes's foster parents began the process of adopting Hughes. As part of this process, Hughes's DNA was compared to Floyd's to establish paternity. It was discovered that Floyd was not Hughes's biological father, a fact that would later keep him from gaining custody of Hughes.

On March 30, 1993, Floyd was released to a halfway house. He began working as a maintenance man at an apartment complex. Not long after, he returned to his old ways. On July 4, 1994, Floyd attacked a woman at the apartment complex where he worked. Floyd hid in the bushes of the apartment complex and attempted to attack the woman with a knife when she came home. He was arrested for the attack on August 19, 1994 and was released on bond that same day.

Kidnapping

After he was released from prison, Floyd tried to regain custody of Michael Hughes. However, due to his lengthy criminal record and the recent finding that he had no biological relation to Hughes, a judge denied Floyd's request.

Floyd took matters into his own hands. On September 12, 1994, Floyd went to the elementary school in Choctaw, Oklahoma, where Hughes was in the first grade. Floyd entered the office of Principal James Davis and demanded to see his son. He told Davis he had a gun and showed the gun to Davis, telling him, "If you don't help me, you won't live."

Davis took Floyd to Hughes, and Floyd drove all three of them into the woods in Davis's pickup truck. There, Floyd handcuffed Davis to a tree and left with Hughes.

It's not clear what happened to Hughes after this. Floyd would claim later that Hughes was safe somewhere, then later changed his story and began to say he had killed Hughes.

Floyd returned to Georgia, committing a carjacking in Atlanta. He was also a patient at Grady Memorial Hospital in Atlanta, Georgia from September 21-29, 1994. Floyd didn't stay long, and in October of 1994 Principal Davis's truck was found near the Love Field Airport in Dallas, Texas, suggesting Floyd had been in the area.

Floyd was ultimately apprehended in Louisville, Kentucky. He was arrested on November 10, 1994 at a Kentucky car dealership where he had just started working two days prior. The arrest was for the kidnapping charge, but Floyd would soon be implicated in the murder of Cheryl Commesso.

Putting the Pieces Together

In March of 1995, Cheryl Commesso's body was finally found on the side of I-275 in Tampa, Florida. Meanwhile, the truck that Floyd had stolen when he kidnapped Davis was sold, and the new owner made a disturbing discovery. A thick envelope stuffed with dozens of pictures was found wedged between the bed of the truck and the gas tank.

Some of the pictures showed Cheryl Commesso being tortured and beaten. Others were photographs of Sharon Marshall dating back to when she was a young girl, showing her in sexually suggestive poses. The pictures of Commesso showed her wearing the same jewelry that was found on her body, and there were also pictures of the inside of a trailer and other items that belonged to Floyd. Finally, one picture showed part of someone's thumb. Investigators were able to match the thumb to Floyd. This, along with the photographs of Marshall and Floyd's belongings, was enough evidence to charge Floyd with murder.

On September 28, 2002, Floyd was convicted of first degree murder. The trial had lasted only 90 days and jurors deliberated for just four hours before reaching a guilty verdict. Floyd had an outburst in the courtroom, claiming the prosecutors had framed him and swearing at the judge.

On November 22, 2002, Floyd was sentenced to death. Judge Nancy Moate Ley read the verdict, acknowledging that Floyd had had a difficult childhood, but his long criminal record and the particularly horrific nature of his crime made it necessary for him to be sentenced to death. It was, according to Ley, "not surprising" that the jury had decided on the death penalty.

Floyd is currently on death row in Union Correctional Institution awaiting execution. Many mysteries still surround Franklin Delano Floyd and the crimes he committed. No one has yet been arrested in the hit-and-run accident that killed Sharon Marshall.

In 2014, DNA evidence was used to discover the true identity of Sharon Marshall, linking her to Sandra Chipman. Finally, the truth about Suzanne Sevakis, the North Carolina girl who had been missing for decades, and Sharon Marshall, the mystery girl Floyd had kidnapped, was revealed—they were the same person.

Floyd would also later confess to murdering Michael Hughes, though there is no proof of this claim and no remains have been found. Floyd was able to identify a location in the woods where he claims he killed Hughes. The truth, however, like so many things about Franklin Delano Floyd, may never be known.

SERIAL KILLER JUANA BARRAZA

MARCUS MOORE

Juana Barraza is perhaps the most famous serial killer in all of Mexico's history. Authorities have attributed the death of up to 48 elderly women in Mexico to Juana, and she was found guilty in 2008 of several murders and was sentenced to a total of 759 years in jail for her crimes. Referred to as Mataviejitas, or Little Old Lady Killer, Juana's killing spree and the subsequent police investigation, became national news in Mexico in 2007 and 2008, and led to widespread pressure on the police department to solve the series of crimes against the nation's most vulnerable members of society.

Background

Juana Barraza, or Juana Dayanara Barraza Samperio, was born on December 27, 1958 in the small rural town of Epazoyucan, Hidalgo, located north of the nation's capital of Mexico City. Her father, Trinidad Barraza, was a local police officer and her mother, Justa Samperio, was a prostitute. Juana's mother left her father shortly after Juana's birth to begin a relationship with a married man named Refugio Samperio, was was Justa's stepfather during her childhood.

Juana reportedly suffered from a difficult and violent childhood, living with an extreme alcoholic for a mother. She was illiterate as a child and was often physically and emotionally neglected by her mother. She would later claim that her mother sold her to a strange man named Jose Lugo when she was only twelve years old for just three beers; the man sexually assaulted Juana repeatedly and she became pregnant with a boy. Juana would eventually have a total of four children, although her oldest son died in a robbery attempt at 24 years old.

Prior to becoming famous for her role as a serial killer, Juana was a relatively little-known wrestler who participated in the amateur circuits of lucha libre, a famous form of Mexican wrestling that involves the use of masks and significant amounts of stage drama. During her career as a wrestler, she performed under the stage name La Dama del Silencio, also known as The Silent Lady in Spanish.

While Juana toured the country as a part of the amateur wrestling circuit in the 1980s and 1990s, she turned to stealing and burglary in 1995 after birthing her fourth child. In 1996, she began robbing elderly people with a friend of hers, setting up a pattern of targeting the elderly that would last throughout her entire criminal career. The two burglars would dress in all-white scrubs and pretend to be nurses in order to gain their victim's trust and access to their homes.

Crimes

Juana's profile as a serial killer was that she consistently targeted elderly women, in their late 60s or older. Many of her victims lived alone and had little contact with local relatives or a strong social circle. Juana would typically befriend the victim, then lure them to their home or a quiet place where she would bludgeon them to death with a heavy object or strangle them with an extension cord that she carried on her person, usually robbing the victim once they were dead.

Juana used several different methods to gain her victims' trust. She would often cruise the streets of poorer neighborhoods, looking for elderly woman who were by themselves and struggling with bags of groceries or other household items. She would then offer to help the elderly women up their set of stairs to their apartments, where she would the kill her victim. Juana would also frequently pose as a government official, complete with an ID badge and government application forms. She would claim that she was going door-to-door to help pensioners apply for their benefits in order to gain their trust and access to their home. She frequently used phone cords, extension cables, tights, or a stethoscope to strangle her victims.

It is suspected that Juana's first victim was Maria de la Luz Gonzalez Anaya, who was murdered on November 25, 2002. Juana gained access to her apartment, likely in order to rob the elderly woman, but ended up killing Maria Gonzalez after the woman made disparaging comments about Juana, angering her and leading to her strangling the victim in a fit of rage.

Several years into her career as a serial killer, Juana Barraza began a romantic relationship with Jose Francisco Torres Herrera, a taxi driver known as El Frijol, or The Bean. Together, the two continued her killing spree and began by targeting Carmen Camila Gonzalez Miguel, an 82-year old wealthy woman in Mexico City. While the pair did successfully kill Carmen and escape, this murder led to a widespread police response and investigation into the existence of a serial killer in Mexico City. Carmen Gonzalez was the mother of Luis Rafael Moreno Gonzalez, a well-known and powerful criminologist. Her death led to increased police patrols, a public information campaign, and a collaboration with French investigators, who had recently detained The Monster of Montmartre, a prominent French serial killer.

Police Investigation

During the early stages of the investigation into a potential serial killer, the chief prosecutor for Mexico City, Bernardo Batiz, publicly said that he thought the killer had "a brilliant mind, quite clever and careful" and that he suspected the killer was adept at gaining the trust of their potential victims prior to killing them. Several officials believed that the killer was posing as a government benefits counselor who established trust by offering to help the victim secure government benefits like health care and welfare.

There was an odd coincidence which confused the police working on the case and led to detectives investigating misleading information that ultimately delayed Juana's capture. Early on, the police noticed that at least three of the women killed by Juana owned a copy of the Boy in Red Waistcoat, a famous painting from the 1700s by French painter Jean-Baptiste Greuze. For some time, police were convinced that the presence of this painting had some important bearing on the case and why the victims were chosen; but, ultimately it became clear that the presence of the painting was mere coincidence and that the police department's focus on this "evidence" was misplaced.

Police were able to determine through their investigation and subsequent in-person interviews that Juana was clinically classified as a psychopath: she did not feel any pain or remorse for actions, and thus had no moral qualms about her actions and their effects. Psychologists say that Juana associated the elderly women that she preyed on with her mother, believing that her actions were a net good because she was removing evil people from the world. Her lack of empathy, combined with her engaging persona and false identity as a government worker, allowed her to gain these women's trust in a small amount of time.

Despite the rash of killings in Mexico City in late 2005 and early 2006, the local police department consistently dismissed any theories of an emerging serial killer and called out such ideas as "media sensationalism." However, police did begin to take reports of a serial killer seriously in November 2005, when they received several witness statements reporting that the killer wore women's clothing, leading them to suspect that the serial killer was actually a transvestite who posed as a woman to gain access to, and trust from, his victims. On one particular occasion, the killer was seen living a victim's house wearing a red blouse.

Once the police department finally did launch a full investigation of the killings, their first action was to launch a city-wide raid of all of the areas frequented by transvestite prostitutes, since they mistakenly believed at that time that the killer was a transvestite who dressed as a female in order to gain the trust of his female victims. A reporter for La Jornada, a popular newspaper in Mexico City, would call the series of raids "ham-fisted" unproductive.

In addition to detaining and questioning all of the city's known transvestite prostitutes, the police also began visiting the local morgue to check fingerprints. They believed that the killer may have committed suicide and that they need only verify the identity of one of the corpses to close the case. This belief would quickly prove to be incorrect.

Despite initial fumbling by the police department and an investigation predicated based upon incorrect assumptions about the killer, the case would soon break open in a very public way. On January 25th, 2006, a suspect was seen fleeing from the home of the now-deceased Ana Maria de los Reyes Alfaro, an 82-year old women living in the Venustiano Carranza section of Mexico City. Ana Alfaro was strangled to death with a stethoscope by Juana Barraza. Luckily for the police, Alfaro was a landlady and one of her new tenants was arriving at her home as Juana attempted to flee the scene of the crime. The tenant nearly bumped into Juana as she rushed out of the building and was the first to see Reyes Alfaro's body. He immediately called the police and was able to provide the description that led to Juana's capture.

In a surprise to both the police, national media, and public, the suspected killer was actually Juana Barraza, a 48 year old amateur wrestler, and a woman that many people would mistake for a kindly grandmother; here was the famed Mexico City serial killer, and the nation was shocked.

Police investigators were initially drawn to the idea of a transvestite serial killer because of composite sketches and witness statements that described the serial killer as a masculine-looking woman. Given these statements and the fact that the vast majority of serial killers are men, they police department completely ignored the possibility that the killer could actually be a "masculine-looking woman," as opposed to a man dressed as a woman.

Despite this initial confusion, police quickly realized that Juana looked remarkably similar to the police sketches that had been composed from witness statements. The more that police learned about Juana, the more that her role as the serial killer made sense. Police initially thought that the killer had to be a man or male transvestite because of the sheer amount of strength required to strangle someone. They thought that it was impossible for a woman possess that much physical strength; however, Juana was no ordinary woman. She was a professional wrestler reportedly capable of bench pressing 200 lbs for multiple sets of ten, a significant sign of strength in any person.

Furthermore, her use of the stethoscope to kill her last victim was in line with witness statements, which had described a government worker with short, dyed-blonde hair and a mole on their face, carrying a stethoscope, benefit forms, and a government ID card.

Once detained, police were quickly able to connect Juana to at least ten other murders using her fingerprints. Mexico City's chief prosecutor at the time, Bernardo Batiz, would tell the media that "Fingerprints match in 10 murder cases, as well as one attempt." In addition, police investigators found several trophies related to the killings in her home, including cutouts of newspaper articles discussing the killings (despite the fact that she is illiterate). Juana admitted to killing Ana Alfaro, but said that she had initially visited the elderly woman's home in order to secure work during laundry and that she killed the woman out of "anger," and not because of any premeditated reason.

Trial

Juana Barraza began her trial for murder in spring 2008, with prosecutors claiming that she was responsible for up to 40 killings over the previous six years. While Juana admitted to killing Ana Alfaro, claiming that she murdered the elderly woman out of anger because she resembled Juana's abusive mother, she claimed that she was innocent of all of the other charges levied against her.

Despite her claims of innocence, Juana was sentenced to prison for 759 years in March 2008, after being found guilty of 11 separate murder charges and an aggravated burglary charge. Given that federal sentences in Mexico are served concurrently and legally the maximum sentence a person can receive is 60 years, it is likely that Juana will die in prison. However, she will be eligible for parole in 2058, when she is 100 years old.

Suspected Victims

Robbery

1995-2001

Juana is suspected of robbing a large, unknown amount of victims during this time period.

Murder

2002

November 24th: Maria de la Luz Gonzalez Anaya (64 years old)

2003

March 2nd: Guillermina Leon Oropeza (84 years old)

July 25th: Maria Guadalupe Aguilar Cortina (86 years old)

October 9th: Maria Duadalupe de la Vega Morales (87 years old)

October 24th: Maria del Carmen Munoz Cote de Galvan (78 years old)

2004

February 20th: Alicia Gonzalez Castillo (75 years old)

February 25th: Andrea Tecante Carreto (74 years old)

March 20th: Carmen Cardona Rodea (76 years old)

March 26th: Socorro Enedina Martinez Pajares (82 years old)

May 24th: Guadalupe Gonzalez Sanchez (74 years old)

June 25th: Esthela Cantoral Trejo (85 years old)

July 1st: Delfina Gonzalez Castillo (92 years old)

July 3rd: Maria Virginia Xelhuatzi Tizapan (84 years old)

July 19th: Maria de los Angeles Cortes Reynoso (84 years old)

August 31st: Margarita Martell Vazquez (72 years old)

September 29th: Simona Bedolla Ayala (79 years old)

October 24th: Maria Dolores Martinez Benavides (70 years old)

November 9th: Margarita Arredondo Rodriguez (83 years old)

November 17th: Maria Imelda Estrada Perez (76 years old)

2005

January 11th: Julia Vera Duplan (60 years old)

February 10th: Maria Elena Mendoza Vallares (59 years old)

April 13th: Maria Elisa Perez Moreno (76 years old)

April 14th: Arturo Patino Barranco (74 years old)

April 19th: Carolina Robledo (79 years old)

April 20th: Ana Maria Velazquez Diaz (62 years old)

June 17th: Celia Villaliz Morales (78 years old)

June 29th: Maria Guadalupe Nunez Almanza (78 years old)

July 5th: Julia Vargas (64 years old)

July 5th: Mario Cruz Flores (84 years old)

July 20th: Emma Armenta Aguayo (80 years old)

August 9th: Emma Reyes Pena (72 years old)

August 11th: Carmen Sanchez Serrano (76 years old)

August 15th: Dolores Concepcion Silva Calva (91 years old)

September 28th: Maria del Carmen Camila Gonzalez Miguel (82 years old)

September 28th: Guadalupe Oliver Contreras (85 years old)

October 18th: Maria de los Angeles Repper Hernandez (92 years old)

2006

January 25th: Ana Maria de los Reyes Alfaro (84 years old)

Juana' Public Response

Juana has repeatedly denied that she is a serial killer, although she has admitted to at least one murder. During her first appearance in court for her trial, she stated "I only killed one little old lady. Not the others. It isn't right to pin the others on me." When she was later asked about her motive for the sole killing that she took responsibility for, she simply said, "I got angry."

Juana has maintained her innocence throughout her trial, verdict and during her current stay in prison, remarking at her verdict, "May God forgive you and not forget me." She has vowed to appeal all but one of the charges she was found guilty of, claiming that her sole killing was a crime of passion against Ana Alfaro on the day she was caught.

BONUS STORY:

Drugs, violence, and bloodshed are three words that one can use to describe one of the most notable female drug traffickers and killers in history. She was ruthless, she was merciless, she did not care who or what was in her way because for her, life was a path that she was destined to walk, no matter how bumpy the road is and no matter how many obstacles and hurdles she had to jump over to get to her final destination. She had killed more people than one can imagine and she had sold more cocaine than one could even dream. She showed the world just how powerful women were, just how powerful she was. The story of this woman is a story full of struggle, death, and betrayal so sit back and tune into the adventures of a woman who was the pioneer behind many of the modern day drug trafficking traditions that ultimately changed the game forever.

Griselda Blanco is a name you may not recognize, but maybe La Madrina, Godmother of Cocaine, or the Black Widow may ring a bell. The story of this notorious drug lord starts when Blanco was born on February 15th, 1943 in Cartagena, a small town with nothing to offer. However since she only stayed here for three years, this was not where Blanco spent most of her childhood days. At the age of three, she moved to Medellín, the same town that the legend Pablo Escobar was raised in, with her mother, Ada Lucía Restrepo. In a town where murders were an everyday occurrence and everyone was riddled with poverty, kids often resorted to committing crimes such as theft or robbery in order to make ends meet. Even worse, with no father figure and an abusive alcoholic mother, Blanco did just that, but even worse. Her rough beginnings were only the backdrop for the crimes she will eventually commit and the person she will eventually become.

At the young age of 11, she and a few of her friends had gone to the rich part of the neighborhood, as compared to the slums in which they lived, to kidnap a 10-year-old boy from a wealthy Colombian family. Together, they attempted to hold the poor boy hostage in the hillside while trying to ransom his parents for money. However, his parents refused to give the money and after a dare from one of her friends, she pointed the gun on the boy's forehead and gave him his fatal shot. He may have been her first kill, but it surely won't be her last.

A few years after this incident, at the age of 14, Blanco ran away from her family after her deadbeat mother's boyfriend had tried to rape her. Alone in the city of Medellín, she resorted to pickpocketing and prostitution in order to keep herself alive. However, she was determined to not just be an unfortunate victim in her story, but instead, a survivor who will viscously claw her way back up to the top, no matter what it'll take. Thus she joined the Medellín Cartel, where she began her career as a small time criminal. Initially, she started to sell marijuana, a much less dangerous drug as compared with what she'll later sell. It was also at this time when she met her husband-to-be, Carlos Trujillo, a street hustler who made a living by selling fake immigration documents. It wasn't soon before they got married and eventually had three children together; Dixon, Uber, and Osvaldo. However their marriage was rather short-lived as she had divorced him, and later reportedly shot her husband over a business dispute. However, this will not be the last time in which she killed someone over a business dispute.

In the mid-1970's, soon after shooting her first husband dead, she met her second husband-to-be, Alberto Bravo, a cocaine trafficker. Slowly transforming from a small time crook to a cocaine dealer, she and Bravo went to America to pursue the classic American dream. Upon arriving in New York, where Blanco had first stayed, they easily and quickly established a cocaine business. Since they were from Colombia, they were directly connected to the source of this drug that would take over this country for decades. This gave them a clear advantage and that advantage was what ultimately gave Blanco and Bravo that edge they needed to finally get walking on the stairs of this dangerous yet strangely exhilarating game of narcotics.

In the beginning, when this whole business was done on a much smaller scale, they would have people, specifically female couriers, carry small amounts of the drug in their suitcases and in their lingerie that Blanco specially designed that would hold small bags of cocaine in the crotch area, but as business grew and their empire extended, they had different plans. New York's drug industry, before Blanco and Bravo had arrived, was run by the mafia, however, despite being new to the game, they instantly took over. Eventually, Blanco ended up having her own personal pilots fly in large quantities of drugs, straight from Colombia to America. Their business grew and grew and she was making millions and millions each month, but with these numbers, came scrutiny from the police.

In April of 1975, she was indicted with 30 of her fellow gang members for a federal drug conspiracy case, which at that time, was the biggest cocaine-related case known. However, before she could even step foot on the court, she had disappeared. "We had her on drug conspiracy charges," Palombo recalls, a member in the Banshee operation in which over 150 kilograms of cocaine was intercepted, "but she was nowhere to be found." Little did they know, she had flown back to Colombia in order to avoid arrest, and the next time she would come back to America, she would come back even stronger than before.

However, before she went back to America to continue her business and empire, she had to rid herself of one of her biggest competitors; her husband. For some time, Blanco had suspected that he was stealing profit from her, and so she decided to settle it once and for all. She met her soon to be dead husband in a parking lot, surrounded by six armed bodyguards, whereas she herself only had a pistol. As the argument got nasty, Blanco took out her pistol and shot Bravo quickly and without missing a beat, she took the Uzi out of his waistband and proceeded to shoot the other six bodyguards. Though she left the scene with a wound on her stomach, she quickly recovered, but her husband and his bodyguards, not so much. This is only the beginning to the ruthless cold blooded murderer that will eventually take over America by storm.

Now returning back to America, she had nobody holding her back as she set foot into the once innocent city of Miami, Florida. The timing of her arrival was just right because, during that time, the local cocaine business was booming due to newly arrived Cuban refugees that have created an underground crime channel. Miami, a city which was now covered in crime, blood, and murder, was the perfect battleground for Blanco to restart her empire, and this time, it'll be bigger and deadlier than before.

She was determined to not just be a part of this drug business, she wanted to be the best, she wanted to own the entire empire. By the late 1970s, Griselda and a couple of her new thugs under the lead of Jorge "Rivi" Ayala, drew up a war plan in which she would kill all of her competition, one by one, until she was the last one standing. Her plan was simple, if she killed all her competition she would be the undisputed queen. Her rules for killing were even more simple, she ordered her assassins to murder everyone, and unlike other more kindhearted criminals, she did not spare women or children, she simply killed them all. If you owed her money and she didn't feel like waiting, she killed you, if she owed you money and she didn't feel like paying you back, she killed you, and if she just didn't like you, she killed you. Her ruthlessness was what truly brought her from being a small time pick-pocket to the godmother of cocaine. The same ruthlessness also brought her a lot of loyal followers because as Palombo said, "She mesmerized people. She could woo you with her acumen and make you a loyal follower. There was also fear: Anybody working for her also knew she wouldn't ask anyone to do what she wouldn't do herself." Best put, she had hundreds of blindly devoted lapdogs, who were ready at her service to do as she wished, and she made them believe that even though she was clearly superior, they both shared a common bond. However, they were far from correct because to Blanco, not only were they easily replaceable, they were also as worthless as a penny on the street.

Fortunately for the godmother, the violence paid off. It wasn't before long that her business swept from coast to coast with over 80 million dollars in profit. This was the beginning of a new era, the Miami drug war, or as some may call it, the Cocaine Cowboy War. Miami, a city that used to be full of retired old people was slowly being transformed into the battlefield between underground crime and the police. As the news of her success spread across the nation, more and more people wanted to be a part of this dangerous yet largely successful business. Their lawlessness and corrupt personality eventually became an epidemic that led to the creation of the CENTAC 26, which was used to hopefully stop these crimes from being committed.

However tension grew as Blanco was mercilessly killing more and more people, and as a result, she gained more and more enemies. In one incident in 1979, a trio of Blanco's assassins were in their van outside of a Miami liquor store and unleashed a spray of machine gun fire at German Jimenez Panesso, a fellow cocaine dealer, as well as one of his subordinates. This attack ultimately killed the two as well as injured two mall employees, but when the police arrived at the crime scene, all they found was an abandoned van. The van itself contained an assortment of different weapons including shotguns, revolvers, and machine guns. The plastic one-way windows on the van also allowed the gunmen to look at the people outside, but not the other way around. This not only brought even more scrutiny to Blanco and her business but also made it apparent and crystal clear that Blanco was not one to be messed with.

Blanco however, was not bothered by the extra attention that was brought to her, instead, she was more concerned with how to expand her already enormous empire. In fact, she enjoyed the attention, as Rivi, one of her many subordinates, said, "She liked to be at war... It was something she enjoyed." Simply put, she wasn't scared of the threats that were thrown at her, in fact, she welcomed them because she knew she would ultimately win, or so she thought.

To just name a few of the people she killed, in 1982, she had ordered Jesus Castro, another fellow rival drug trafficker, to be killed for insulting and offending one of her sons, however, the assassins missed, but in the midst of the gunfire, one of the bullets hit Castro's 2-year-old son. Only about a year later, she had ordered Alfred and Gabriel Lorenzo, a married couple that also happened to deal cocaine in the city of Miami, Florida, to be killed. Rivi was ordered to be the head of the mission and while he and a couple of other fellow thugs killed them in one room, they left Lorenzo's children alone in the other room. Unlike Blanco, Rivi refused to kill the children as they were innocent in this whole ordeal.

As much as she loved being at war, after several murder attempts, she was forced to flee. In one case, Jaime, a rival drug lord of Blanco and the nephew of Bravo, and his two Colombian imported gunmen would wait at the mall that she often visited for an attempt to kill her. Even though it meant accepting defeat, she relocated to California in 1984 in order to avoid death, but the story does not stop there and neither did the threats.

For a while, she attempted to lie low in Irvine, California, but her luck eventually ran out. With Jaime looking for her and the police also following her tracks, Blanco was pressed into a corner with no moves to make. At the age of 42, she was most definitely getting old and her age definitely put her at a disadvantage as her enemies and opponents were much more young and much more fit. On February 20th, 1985, Palombo and the rest of her team, broke into the house that Blanco and her mother and youngest son was staying at and arrested her while she was upstairs in her bedroom. According to Palombo, when they barged into the door of her bedroom she was laying in bed reading the bible as she had recently turned to religion for help since she was going through a tough time. None a doubt, it was a humiliating defeat for Blanco to begin with, but the defeat was even more humiliating after Palombo had kissed her on the cheek after he caught her. This was due to a bet Palombo had with his fellow agents in the case where he promised to seal the capture with a kiss.

Immediately the judge for the case ordered that Blanco be held without bail and later sentenced Blanco to more than a decade behind bars. News reports and articles flooded the nation with headlines saying that the demise of the 'Queen of Cocaine' finally came. Little did they know that the 'Queen of Cocaine' was going to reign for much longer, even if it meant that she would have to do it behind bars. However running a business behind bars was much harder than it seems, so she had to enlist some help.

Charles Cosby was just a starting coke dealer who moved cocaine by the ounce when he saw for himself the arrest of Blanco. After seeing Blanco being arrested for 150 kilos of coke, he was mesmerized and inspired. Like Michael Jordan to a basketball fan, Blanco instantly became an inspiration and idol for Cosby. After a plea from Blanco, she was able to secure her sentence to 20 years and to an all women jail called FCI Dublin, which was only 20 miles from Oakland, where Cosby resided. As Cosby said himself, "Griselda was the connection of all connections," and through a common friend that was once a runner for Blanco, he was able to get into contact with his idol.

Surprisingly so, Blanco agreed to this, and after numerous exchanges of phone calls, notes, and letters, they finally came face to face. During the visiting hours, Cosby arrived at the jail in which Blanco temporarily called her home, and they did more than just talk. In fact, upon meeting him, Blanco had given Cosby a long passionate kiss on the mouth, only shortly before getting right down to business. Once they sat down, Blanco's straightforwardness shocked Cosby, as she began the talk by asking him, "How much money do you need for you and your family to be comfortable?" Cosby, knowing that Blanco needed his help as much he needed hers, threw out an enormous sum that he initially expected had to be negotiated; he told her 50 keys, code for 50 kilograms. To his surprise, she immediately accepted his offer with no further negotiation.

Within three days, a Latino woman showed up at the front door of Cosby's house saying that she had a special delivery from 'Godmother.' Cosby immediately knew who it was from and upon opening, he knew that he was going to be a millionaire in not time, and he was right. And he was right, with these 50 kilos of cocaine, he was able to become a millionaire in less than a month, with all his success attributed to none other than the queen of cocaine.

However, Cosby's repayment for all that Blanco had given him was a little more than just out of the ordinary. Blanco would pay $1500 to the guards of her jail cell every time Cosby went to visit so they could have sex in the multipurpose room in the back of the jail. Furthermore, Cosby became Blanco's protege and managed her multi-billion empire and business. Since Blanco had set everything up for Cosby, he didn't have to do much, all he had to do was fly to different places and shake a few hands and make the deals that Blanco wants him to make. Best put by Cosby himself, "All I had to do was fly around the country and meet with distributors. Every time I shook a hand, I made $1 million." Through this system, Blanco was able to continue her business despite being trapped behind bars and likewise, her ever-growing list of enemies did not stop.

In 1992, her son Osvaldo was killed in Medellín and when the news finally got to her in jail, she vowed for revenge and she did indeed get it. The killers were later caught and tortured for days before being given the sweet release of death. However not everything that Blanco did was successful, in fact, she ran into some legal trouble after a few years.

In 1995, she was being indicted for three murders, with one of the main witnesses being Rivi, her hitman back in the days. According to Cosby, she fell into a nervous panic attack when she heard that Rivi was testifying against her and even said that, "Rivi has enough dirt on me to bury me 10 times." As Sergeant Al Singleton, one of the many other people involved in this case, said, "Griselda was our John Gotti and Rivi was our Sammy 'The Bull' Gravano." In a desperate attempt to save herself, she told Cosby to give a note that said "jfk 5m ny" to Dixon. Upon questioning from Cosby, Blanco confessed that she was planning to get Dixon to hire kidnappers for five million dollars to kidnap Kennedy Jr. and ransom him in exchange for the freedom of Blanco. Though Cosby knew from the beginning that Blanco was something else, he in no way expected a plan this insane and dangerous. Though Cosby initially refused to even relay the message, after further persuasion and Blanco going as far to comparing Cosby to Rivi for betraying her, he finally gave Dixon the message.

Soon after Dixon got the message, four Colombian men were hired to perform the plan. Soon after arriving in New York City, the four kidnappers took no time to start their plan and Cosby still shaken, was forced to stay with them in the safe house in order to oversee the mission. They soon moved to the Tribeca neighborhood, in which the kidnappers staked-out the Kennedy residence. However Cosby, in fear of being caught, went back to California to remove himself from the situation. However, for weeks, the kidnappers had no luck in even encountering Kennedy, but one day the tides turned to their favor. They spotted Kennedy walking his dog outside the building and were quick to take hold of his opportunity. However, none of them got close enough to even harm, let alone kidnap Kennedy. One of the four kidnappers did get close enough to pet the dog's head, but after seeing an NYPD squad car pass by them, the plan was called off.

At this point, Cosby had enough of the scariness and unpredictableness that came with working with a drug mastermind like Blanco. Fed up with the sleepless nights and constant worrying, he flew to Florida to testify against Blanco, the very woman who gave him everything he had. With two witnesses stacked against Blanco, everyone thought that that would be the end of her, however, in an unexpected turn of events, Blanco was safe.

Though he had agreed to testify, he purposely understated the mass success and sum of money that came with Blanco's business, in an example he said, "I said she was making $2 million when it was actually 50 times that." Though this did initially throw them off, nonetheless, with Rivi as the other witness, the attorneys were fairly certain that they'll be able to hammer down Blanco with lifetime charges, however, the same people who dug a hole for her to fall into were the same people who dragged her back up.

In the form of a scandal, both Rivi and Cosby ultimately saved Blanco. During Cosby's deposition, he had claimed that he had sex with one of the secretaries of the state attorney's office, allowing the prosecutors to question the credibility of Cosby's testimony. And with that, Cosby, an important witness of the case, was thrown out. However the attorneys still had Rivi, their star witness, or so they thought. Turns out, Rivi had an extended phone-sex affair with the same secretary, resulting in his testimony being thrown out as well. With the two prime witnesses being discredited through these technicalities the entire case collapsed and to Blanco's luck, she was set to only serve her remaining years then leave. However, it is speculated that Rivi and Cosby did all of this not to save Blanco, but to save themselves since they knew snitches get stitches. Furthermore, Blanco was known to torture and kill betrayers so it was most likely the best for both Rivi and Cosby to dissociate themselves from the case.

Finally and at last, in 2004, Blanco was finally free to go, finally free to leave the four walls that have been haunting her every night and day. She was then deported back to her homeland of Colombia, which was in a way better than her previous living condition, however, on the other hand, she was being deported back to the very home country where her sons were murdered in. It was safe to say that there was no way that even a woman like Blanco could feel safe being back there.

As Palombo said, "If I was getting deported to the country where my sons were whacked, I wouldn't feel too comfortable." Though she had enemies everywhere and around the world, Medellín was probably one of the most dangerous places for her to stay at.

Mant predicted that within days of leaving jail, Blanco would be killed by enemies as she had so many. As Nelson Andreu, one of the homicide detectives on Blanco's case says, "It's surprising to all of us that she had not been killed sooner because she had made a lot of enemies. When you kill so many and hurt os many people like she did, it's only a matter of time before they find you and try to even the score." However, as she always does, she beats the odds and survives for a few more years. In 2006, Cocaine Cowboys, a movie about the drug war in Miami, made its debut directed by Billy Corben, but the star, Blanco, was still nowhere to be seen, it was literally as if she had vanished into thin air, never to be seen again.

However, in May of 2007, she was spotted at the Bogatá airport and a picture of her was sent directly to Albert Spellman via email. It's safe to say that everyone expected Blanco to have died by now, since all the odds were stacked up against her, but that was not the case, Blanco was not only a good fighter, but a good hider, and for that, she survived for a few more years before she met her inevitable demise. Though she had put her criminal past behind her, the enemies that she has made were not left behind, but instead, they were fast approaching.

Her end came in an almost ironic way actually, as she was killed by a method of killing that she herself invented. On September 2nd, 2013, at the age of 69, she was killed in a motorcycle drive-by outside of a butcher shop in which two assassins drove by on motorcycles, unleashed a cloud of machine gun fire, then drove away. Two fatal bullets to the head were all it took for the end of someone who had paved the way for future. This method of killing was first used by Blanco in order to kill her rival drug lords since it was fast and effective.

This was a classic example of living by the sword, and dying by the sword, a rather fitting death for someone like her. No one even recognized the dead corpse on the floor as Blanco until her very own daughter in law saw her. Though no one on the streets recognized her, she went down with an empire attributed to her, which is more than what most people ask for.

Griselda Blanco was a woman who defied the odds and became more than just what she born as. She was the perfect example of how through hard work, brutal mercilessness, and strong will, one could be able to achieve much more than they were set out to. Her legacy lives way beyond her death, as she had completely changed the system and set the bar so high that few even nowadays could reach. She is the perfect example of how you can both be scared of someone for their ruthlessness, but at the same time admire their remarkable cunningness. Even more than that, she is a timeless criminal for even a decade after she had died, there are still people talking about her, movies being written about her, and people who still look up to her as inspiration.

She showed the world that a small time girl from a city in the middle nowhere could end up becoming a nationally known high profile criminal that had hundreds upon hundreds of people plotting against her, but at the same time, hundreds upon hundreds of people working for her. In many ways, she was a survivor, she had endured the pains of her rough childhood and somehow still ended up achieving the success that she did.

Her life had often been the subject of many documentaries, movies, and books for her life played itself like a movie with its interesting plot twists and traits about her character that would shock the audience. Some of these things are rather hard to believe, even for someone as unpredictable as Blanco. For example, there were rumors that not only was she a bisexual, but that she often forced both men and women to have sex with her at gunpoint as well as participate in orgies. Slightly less shocking and rather fitting for her character, she was also addicted to an unrefined type of cocaine that was smokeable, called "bazooka." This drug was (and still is) very popular in Colombia, making it very easy for Blanco to get ahold of it. However despite her horrible acts of violence and weird hobbies, she considered herself a religious person as Cosby said, "She found religion in [her] later years, [but] at the same time, you can't bring a Bible to a gunfight."

Furthermore, drugs and murder were only a few of her criminal acts, since she was also a thief. Legend has it that not only were most of her most prized possessions stolen, she had actually stolen them herself.

In that list was a MAC 10 machine pistol that was embellished in emeralds and gold, as well as a set of pearls that was stolen from the First Lady of Argentina, Eva Perón. Even worse, she had owned a tea cup set once used by Queen Elizabeth smuggled out of the Buckingham Palace itself. However as one may guess, these crimes were not at all even comparable to her drug crimes, reportedly, she was in charge of smuggling over 3,400 lbs. of cocaine into the US a month, which hand in hand, also brought a large number of murders. For a more conservative estimate, she had killed anywhere from 40-50 people, however on the high end, she could've easily killed over 200 people, and within these numbers, she had killed many people who were close to her, including her three husbands, making her the deadliest of Black Widows.

She had truly proved that women drug traffickers could do just as much if not even more than male drug traffickers, as Abreu says, "Griselda was worse than any of the men that were involved [in the drug trade]." She was a classic example of the phrase "rags to riches" since she literally was raised in the slums of a forgotten town and turned into the hometown of a forever remembered criminal. Her story was one that was filled with lovers turned haters, backstabbers, but also of glory. The world was her oyster and through violence, she was finally able to find the pearl inside, even if it was deadly. Though fate had caused her end, fate had also made it so that her end will never be forgotten.

Whether you think it was the environment and circumstances that gave birth to such a notorious criminal that eventually spawned an empire so vast that it'll last for decades or that it was etched into Blanco's skin that she become such a person, everyone can agree that Blanco was definitely one of the most notable drug traffickers in recent history.

SERIAL KILLER PETER SUTCLIFFE

BRUCE CANDELO

<u>The Yorkshire Ripper</u>

The Yorkshire Ripper was- is- perhaps the most famous British serial killer, aside from his Victorian namesake. His crimes gripped the nation over a five year period, starting in 1975. But behind the media image created for him was a man called Peter Sutcliffe, a normal man from the accounts of all who knew him. He first worked as a gravedigger, before moving on to regular jobs as a salesman, a factory worker, and finally an HGV driver. Nothing out of the ordinary.

Sutcliffe's story is one of inept policing, media frenzy and unrelenting brutality- and insanity. When initially apprehended, Sutcliffe claimed that he had been ordered to murder prostitutes by no less an authority than God himself. Because of his string of crimes, Sutcliffe has been imprisoned for almost the entirety of his adult life. He has no chance of ever being released.

What made him famous?

The murders took place over the course of five years, and grabbed the public's attention, in particular the murders of women who were not prostitutes. His victims were invariably women, mostly young women; almost all were stripped to some degree, and almost all had been murdered with some combination of a hammer, a knife and a screwdriver. Everything pointed to the work of a serial killer.

Besides the modus operandi, the bodies of the victims also pointed to a depraved murderer. Many had been toyed with after their death, slashed with knives or glass. One had been raped. As can be imagined, the murders captured the public's attention because of their depravity and violence. National newspapers complained of how long it was taking police forces to catch the killer.

In fairness to the police, however, they had been led down the wrong trail by faked evidence. Incredibly, the case was put back- maybe even by several years- by the fact that a member of the public decided to send letters and voice messages to both the media and the police force investigating the Ripper. The perpetrator of the hoax has since been named 'Wearside Jack', because of his distinctive Wearside accent.

In the tapes, he said: "I'm Jack. I see you are still having no luck catching me. I have the greatest respect for you, George, but Lord! You are no nearer catching me now than four years ago when I started. I reckon your boys are letting you down, George. They can't be much good, can they?" Based on the accent of the man in the tape, the police assumed that the man they were hunting was from the Sunderland area; Sutcliffe sounded nothing like him.

What took so long?

The case was being investigated by West Yorkshire Police, the regional authority. They were widely criticised by the media and the government for their inadequate treatment of Sutcliffe's case. Even though the search for the Ripper was the biggest undertaken by any police force in the UK until that point, they had failed catch the killer, largely because of their own reluctance to act on suspicions and the leads they had found. And most remarkably, he had been under their noses all along.

Sutcliffe was interviewed time and time again by police in their search for the Ripper. He had been flagged up as suspicious, but nothing had been done, largely because his accent did not match the one that could be heard in the Wearside Jack tapes. Despite that discrepancy, one junior police officer named Andy Laptew had been particularly convinced that Sutcliffe was his man.

"I wasn't happy with Peter Sutcliffe, there were a lot of alarm bells ringing," he told an interviewer in a BBC documentary. "The reason we actually went to see Sutcliffe was because his vehicle had been sighted in three separate red light areas. He had a striking resemblance to the photo-fit of the woman who was attacked in Buslingthorpe Lane, in Leeds. He had a gap in his teeth which again was indicative of the attacker of two of the women who were killed," Laptew said.

Even his job was in the suspect occupation group, since Sutcliffe was an HGV driver at the time. Despite how well Sutcliffe matched the suspect, however, the police force was (for some reason) reluctant to act on their suspicions. "I said to my colleague, 'why don't we bring him in?" and he said 'no, we have been told specifically: do not bring anybody in'," Laptew said in his interview.

He went on, "In fact, I'll tell you what happened. I took it direct to Dick Holland." Holland was the Superintendent in charge of the enquiry. But Holland was also reluctant to act on Laptew's hunch, despite how well Sutcliffe matched all descriptions and even the photo-fit. His reasoning was that Sutcliffe was from Bradford, a city with a completely different accent to the one they had heard in the fake voice messages. "Then (Holland) said, 'If anybody mentions the photo-fits to me again, they will be doing traffic for the rest of their service.' I could have crawled under the crack in the door."

In total, the police force interviewed a grand total of more than 40,000 people in their search for the Ripper. The vast majority of these were interviewed in the Wearside area, based on the voice of Wearside Jack. The real Ripper lived in Bradford, over 70 miles away. The fact that so much police time was wasted, and several lives lost because of one false lead, puts the Wearside Jack tapes at the top of the list of most damaging hoaxes in the search for any killer.

The beginnings of an obsession

While the police carried on with their manhunt in entirely the wrong part of the country, the Ripper carried on murdering women. For a description of his crimes, Sutcliffe himself is a remarkable source. He has spoken to the press and made highly descriptive confessions which leave no doubt about either his guilt or his capability of doing evil things. He begins his confession to police by explaining how his obsession with killing prostitutes began, and how eventually his hatred transformed into the desire 'to find a prostitute to make it one more less' as often as he could.

He went into gruesome detail, about each and every one of the crimes he had committed. He first described his assault of Wilma McCann, a prostitute local to Leeds. He said that actually, at first, he didn't realise she was a prostitute; all he knew was that she was thumbing a lift. But when she asked him if he 'wanted business', he 'decided to go with her'.

He then describes her impatience with him- he 'was expecting it to be a bit romantic', but she had changed her tone and asked 'what are we waiting for? Let's get on with it!' Sutcliffe described how he was put off, and Wilma stormed off to find another customer. But then, suddenly, he was overcome with rage- he ran after her, wanting to hit her.

He asked her not to go, to which she shouted back at him: 'Oh, you can f***ing manage it now, can you?!' This only made Sutcliffe angrier, and she carried on up the hill. In a fit of rage, he went back to his car, where he had stored his toolbox in the trunk. He found his hammer, and took it with him.

After eventually convincing her that he was ready, Peter got her to stop- but rather than doing what Wilma expected, Peter hit her brutally with the hammer. She crumpled to the ground, and he ran back to his car in a panic. He sat in the car for a while, wondering what he should do, when he noticed her arm moving.

He realised that to get away with what he'd already done, he would have to finish the job. So, he went back to his toolbox in the trunk, to pick out a carving knife. Why he had a carving knife in his toolbox is unclear, especially since he claimed that he committed the murder on the spur of the moment. That being said, the wounds inflicted on the victim matched what Sutcliffe described.

The Ripper's Spree

It was this murder which spurred Sutcliffe's hatred of prostitutes, in order to justify to himself what he had done to Wilma. According to the man himself, his next murder was not long after the first; this time around, he searched specifically for a prostitute that he felt would be an easy victim. He went back to the same city, Leeds, and picked up another woman, killing her with the same hammer that he had used to kill Wilma.

Sutcliffe said that he wasn't sure, but that he still may have had the same hammer in his toolbox by the time he was finally caught. It could have been another hammer that he says he bought specifically for the purpose of killing. Besides his hammer and his knife, he frenziedly attacked this second woman with a screwdriver to make sure she was dead.

All of the other attacks meld into one long, horrible narrative. His third victim he killed with a hammer and a box cutter, which he recalls he later lent to somebody. At this point, Sutcliffe said, 'killing prostitutes became an obsession' that he couldn't stop, 'like some sort of a drug.' His next victim was the one that grabbed national headlines and made the public pay attention, since she was only sixteen years of age, and wasn't even a prostitute.

In October, Sutcliffe murdered Jean Jordan, this time in Manchester. He murdered her in the exact same way as his previous victims, and left her for dead under a row of bushes. A few days later, he realised, the case had not been featured in the news; so incredibly, he decided that he could go back to the scene of the crime to retrieve the £5 note he had given her. But on not being able to find the note, Sutcliffe was "cursing the girl and [his] luck", and decided to take it out on Jordan's body.

He tried cutting off her head with a blunt hacksaw, but gave up quickly; he then took a pane of broken glass and slashed at her exposed stomach, which ruptured. Sutcliffe said in his confession that it "made [him] reel back and immediately vomit... it was horrendous." Realising that he was achieving nothing, he kicked her a few times and drove away.

His next victim, Yvonne Pearson, he hadn't even had to search for: she, not knowing who he was, had come to him. Again, he hit her with his hammer. This time however, a car pulled up next to his as he was dragging her away, and he had to hide with Yvonne- who was still alive- behind an abandoned sofa. This was the murder that suggested even to Peter that he was descending into madness, since after stuffing her throat and mouth full with straw and grass, to keep her quiet, he apologised to her... Even though she had already died.

These were just the first few victims of a number which eventually reached thirteen in total. This, also, is not counting the number of girls that he attacked but who survived. Other victims, he raped before he killed, and soon after his murder of Yvonne Pearson Sutcliffe started feeling an urge to kill any women, not just prostitutes. This, he described, was likely to lead him to be caught, but that in his subconscious mind this was what he really wanted.

Each of the murders that followed was increasingly reckless. The last two were murdered in broad daylight on suburban streets, as the victims walked home. Sutcliffe leapt from his car and beat them, in the middle of the sidewalk, before dragging them to a nearby yard to mutilate their bodies. In each of the last murders, members of the public seemed to get closer and closer to catching Sutcliffe in the act- but fortunately for him, they never did.

Arrest

Unbelievably, Sutcliffe was never apprehended during any of his crimes or in the process of disposing of one of his victims. He managed to completely avoid detection throughout his spree, and was only captured by chance.

Sutcliffe had had many prior scrapes with the police. Way back in 1969, he had assaulted a prostitute he had met during a search for another prostitute who had supposedly tricked him out of money. He got a lift from his friend to St Paul's Road, where he knew her to be; leaving the car, he walked out of sight. A few minutes later, he ran back to his friend, and asked him to make a quick getaway. In a later statement, Sutcliffe said that he told his friend: "I got out of the car, went across the road and hit her. The force of the impact tore the toe off the sock and whatever was in it came out. I went back to the car and got in it."

The prostitute informed police of the incident, and that she had seen the registration of Sutcliffe's friend's car. He was tracked down the next day, and interviewed. He admitted to having hit the woman, but denied using anything but his hand to hit her with. Fortunately for Sutcliffe, the woman didn't want to press charges since she was a known prostitute, and her husband was jailed for assault at the time.

This was just the beginning of Sutcliffe's terrifying spree. While this first victim was lucky, the 13 others were not as lucky; this first crime represented Sutcliffe growing in confidence, and hatred, and it hadn't been long until he learned how to kill. Unfortunately, it had taken police over five years to learn how to stop him.

During the police's search for the Ripper, they had interviewed Sutcliffe an incredible nine times. He was only finally apprehended when he was pulled over by police for driving with fake number plates in January 1981, long after his last murder. He was stopped by police, who had initially noticed that he was driving with a known prostitute, but the police check on his plates led the police to take him in for questioning.

The police noticed that he matched many of the descriptions of the Ripper provided by victims and witnesses, and so decided to question him in relation to the crimes. Police obtained warrants to search his house, and question his wife, and all evidence pointed towards Sutcliffe's guilt. After two days of highly intensive questioning, Sutcliffe confessed to committing the crimes. Based on what he said, the police found a knife, a length of rope and his famous hammer which he had discarded when pulled over by police.

He showed no emotion at all, apart from during the description of one murder, of a girl who was only 16 years old. He was accused of the murder of many women, although he denied the murder of one particular woman, Joan Harrison; it was later found that he had not murdered her, after all. After his confessions, which caused an intense stir in the media, he admitted that he felt he had been driven to murder by the voice of God.

Prison time

The case against Sutcliffe was open and shut. Because of his confessions, neither the courts nor the public were in any doubt that he had perpetrated the crimes of the last five years. However, he did try to convince the judge and jury that he deserved a reduced sentence, owing to a diagnosis of paranoid schizophrenia that he had received. However, he was unsuccessful, and was jailed for 20 consecutive life sentences.

Sutcliffe was jailed over 35 years ago, and has turned 70 years old since his arrest and imprisonment. He was first sent to a prison on the Isle of Wight, an island off the south coast of England. But only three years after being imprisoned, he was transferred to a psychiatric facility called Broadmoor. Broadmoor is famous in the U.K. as a high-security psychiatric hospital, which houses only around 200 people at any one time. While there, people like Sutcliffe receive psychiatric mediation and psychotherapy.

Sutcliffe remained at Broadmoor throughout his sentence, until August 2016 when he was transferred to Frankland Prison in Durham. The public feared that this suggested that he would eventually be released altogether, although Secretary of State for Justice Jack Straw told the House of Commons that there were "no circumstances in which this man will be released".

Sutcliffe's time spent imprisoned has not been happy. He was attacked by a fellow prisoner at Broadmoor, Paul Wilson, in 1996; Wilson had gone into Sutcliffe's room on the pretence of borrowing a videotape before attempting to strangle him, before two other inmates- including another serial killer, Kenneth Erskine- intervened.

Just a year later, Sutcliffe suffered another attack. This time, the attacker had more success. Ian Kay had intended to attack Peter with a razor embedded in a toothbrush. "I was going to ... walk into the room and cut his jugular vein on both sides and wait there until he was dead," Kay admitted to court.

"Killing has always been in my mind, ever since I've been here [at Broadmoor]. In hindsight, I should have straddled him and strangled him with my bare hands... He said God told him to kill thirteen women, and I say the devil told me to kill him because of that." But rather than attack him with the razor, Kay stabbed him repeatedly with a pen. Sutcliffe was blinded in his left eye, and his vision in his right eye was severely damaged.

In 2003, Sutcliffe fell ill and it was discovered that he had developed diabetes during his time at Broadmoor. In 2007, he was attacked again by Patrick Sureda who attempted to blind him in his other eye. Sutcliffe was sat in the dining hall, eating his lunch, when Patrick lunged at him with a regular cutlery knife. He missed, as Sutcliffe lunged backwards, and the blade stabbed him in the cheek instead.

What about Wearside Jack?

While Sutcliffe was in prison, the hoaxer behind the Wearside Jack tapes was also apprehended. In 2005, a review of cold-case files led the police to a man named John Humble was found to have sent the tapes. The tapes were sent in 1978, which makes the police's work all the more impressive- and made Humble 59 years old by the time he was finally tracked down.

By the time of his later life, Humble was a rapidly aging alcoholic. According to police reports, it took several hours for him to sober up enough after his arrest to actually submit to questioning. In explanation for what he had done, Humble claimed that he was inspired in equal parts by a desire for notoriety and a burning hatred of the police force, in relation to an incident earlier in his life where he was arrested for assaulting a police officer. Humble was jailed for nine years for perverting the course of justice, but was released after just four.

He had been a labourer his entire life, and had attempted suicide numerous times due to both guilt and what he felt had been a failed life. He told a national newspaper after his release that it had all been a prank, but it had gone too far, and that he hadn't realised the extent to which his hoax had affected the investigation.

Sonia Sutcliffe

Alongside the story of Peter Sutcliffe is the story of his wife, Sonia. Incredibly, Sonia stayed married to Peter for over a decade after his imprisonment. It was only in 1997 that she remarried a local hairdresser that she had met. Supposedly, Sonia had never known that her husband was a murderer despite his five year spree; the only two people who know the truth are Sonia and Peter themselves.

Sonia has won several high-profile cases against newspapers who she claimed had libelled her. She famously won £600,000 (around $1million adjusted with inflation) from the satirical magazine Private Eye, prompting the editor to claim: "If this is justice, I'm a banana." On appeal, she was only awarded a tenth of the initial settlement. Using the money, she moved into a new flat with her new husband in 1997, still living in the same area of Yorkshire as she had all those years ago. In many other cases of British serial killers, the house that they used to occupy is often bought by the council and demolished, or otherwise razed to the ground. This is to prevent shrines or museums popping up to exploit the sick fame of the murderer who used to live there.

It would have seemed that the perfect opportunity to do just that had come up when they moved out, but neither Sonia nor Peter wanted to sell their old home. In fact, Sonia Sutcliffe and her new husband moved back to the house that she lived in with Peter all those years ago in 2005. Through all the years since she had moved out, she had refused to sell the house- although if Peter did agree, the money wouldn't go to him, but to the Legal Aid Trust, a body that helps fund attorneys for those who can't afford them.

The motive may have been financial, since the property is worth at least half a million dollars and property prices in the UK increase consistently year on year, and Peter would probably never agree to losing half of that value. Their reasoning one way or the other is up for debate, but either way, it's difficult to imagine how Sonia can comfortably live there.

As British newspaper the Daily Express put it- "To this day she parks her car in the garage where Sutcliffe stored the 30 weapons, including hammers, spanners and screwdrivers, he used to murder 13 women in a six-year killing spree. She cooks her meals in the kitchen that houses the sink in which he once washed the bloodied clothes he wore while carrying out his depraved crimes."

Moreover, Sonia still visits Peter in prison, despite her having remarried. Peter has complained to the press that she doesn't visit him as often as she used to, and blames Sonia's new husband for the development- Peter claims that he's jealous and possessive. Even so, she still visits him month by month.

Yet more killings?

The worst thing about Sutcliffe is that even since being put in prison, the number of women he is suspected of having murdered keeps rising. Since being put in jail, Sutcliffe has been interviewed in connection with another 17 unsolved cases which are strikingly similar to the attacks he has admitted to.

Many of the list of unsolved cases involve hammer attacks, which were one of Sutcliffe's trademarks. One of the attacks was on Tracy Browne, who was attached in 1975 at the age of just 14. She was hit repeatedly with a hammer in the small town of Silsden, in West Yorkshire- in other words, in the exact same area as Sutcliffe's other attacks. She is still alive today, perhaps because of good fortune: she claims that her attacker was scared off by a passing car's headlights.

Another attack, from a year prior, is also thought to have been the handiwork of Sutcliffe. Gloria Wood was older than many of the other victims, at 28 years old; she too was hit with a claw hammer, by a man who she later described to police as bearing similarities to the Ripper. The man had offered to help her with her shopping bags before brutally attacking her. A third victim linked to Sutcliffe was Maureen (or Mo) Lea, who was also hit with a hammer- she was also beaten and stabbed with a sharpened screwdriver, just like other victim of Sutcliffe. That attack took place in late 1980, just a year before Sutcliffe's arrest.

Sutcliffe has not been charged with any more murders since he was put in prison. Considering that his sentence will see him die in jail, there seems little need other than closure for the victims of these crimes to investigate the cases.

www.ingramcontent.com/pod-product-compliance
Lightning Source LLC
Chambersburg PA
CBHW051843130726
47987CB00002B/666